4.26.78

Archilochus of Paros

ARCHILOCHUS
OF
PAROS

by
H. D. Rankin
The University, Southampton

NOYES CLASSICAL STUDIES

NOYES PRESS
PARK RIDGE, NEW JERSEY

Published in the United States by
NOYES PRESS
Noyes Building
Park Ridge, New Jersey 07656

Library of Congress Cataloging in Publication Data

Rankin, H   D
    Archilochus of Paros.

    (Noyes classical studies)
    Bibliography: p.
    Includes index.
    1. Archilochus. 2. Poets, Greek—Biography.
I. Title.
PA3873.A77R3   884'.01   77-6157
ISBN 0-8155-5053-7

Written for Anne

PREFACE

My interest in Archilochus goes back many years, but it was in 1972 that I was led to concentrate this interest by the needs of a fourth year honours class in Monash University. Editions like that of Lasserre and Bonnard, Paris (1958), which is full of intelligent and stimulating ideas, and that of Tarditi, Rome (1968), a marmoreally lucid and restrained assessment of the fragments, made the task of studying the available texts not only much easier, but extremely enjoyable. Consequently I soon found myself investigating the surprisingly copious store of periodical literature which had accumulated on the subject of this poet since the end of the last century. After I had added a stone or two to this cairn of criticism, I felt inclined to pursue the matter further, and the following chapters are the outcome.

The emergence of the new and extensive Cologne fragment (Col Pap inv 7511) has given great impetus to the study of Archilochus, and even as I write these words, I am sure that articles are being written about it, adding to those which have appeared so abundantly since its publication by R. Merkelbach and M. L. West in 1974. This Cologne Epode has generated two main lines of debate: first, whether or not it is genuinely a composition of Archilochus; secondly, if it is (or has at least genuine associations with an Archilochean work), is it correct to think that the poet was really talking about real people in this uninhibited way, or were his words merely ritual obscenities directed at unreal persons? Further, were the experiences mentioned in this poem his own, or fantasied? These problems have important implications for the general interpretation of the poet's remaining works.

My view of Archilochus is that he was a poet whose emotions were deeply enmeshed in the material of his own thoughts and experiences, and I do not exclude the idea that he was talking about himself and actual persons. Others write interestingly on the other side, and I have discussed some of their views in the additional notes at the end of the book. There are other writings which I have not mentioned because the manuscript was in the process of publication before they appeared, or before I could obtain them. I shall not list them all, but I should like to mention E. Degani's *Lirici Greci*, Florence (1977), and his *Poeti Greci*

vii

Giambici ed Elegiaci, Milan (1977), both of which contain valuable material on the new poem and its implications for interpretative criticism of Archilochus. There is also J. Henderson's *The Maculate Muse*, New Haven (1975) which I was not able to see in time to take account of its conclusions in my fifth chapter.

I wish to thank Faber and Faber Limited, London, and New Directions Publishing Corporation, New York, for permitting me to quote Ezra Pound's poem, 'Papyrus'. I am grateful also to Jonathan Cape Limited, London, and Random House Incorporated, New York, for allowing me to quote from Peter Wiles' translation of Roger Vailland's *The Law*; also to A. P. Watt and Son, London, and Macmillan Publishing Company Incorporated, New York, for permission to quote from *Autobiographies* by W. B. Yeats.

I am grateful to my colleague Fred Williams for his considered and characteristically acute advice about the manuscript, saving me from many errors. He is certainly not responsible for anything erroneous that remains. I also thank Mrs. Sheila James for her patience and unfailing goodwill in typing the manuscript. I should like to acknowledge also the help of the Noyes Press in the person of Mrs. Martha Gillies for the skill and efficiency which she has directed to the task of transforming a typescript into a book.

Southampton   *H. D. Rankin*
                                                                June, 1977

TABLE OF CONTENTS

I

HIS REPUTATION IN ANTIQUITY

His fragments leave us in no doubt that Archilochus as poet and as man was turbulent and fierce. Small though most of them are in individual extent, they assure his importance in the history of poetry. He made his poetry about politics, war, wandering, love and the resentment that he felt when his sense of personal honour was injured or affronted. Like some Odysseus goaded by passion[1] and bitter anger rather than guided by affection and prudent intelligence, he wandered through a world of beauty and suffering, elation and despair. His monsters were those obstacles to personal fulfilment in public life and in private affection which arose from the facts of his own mixed origins and the political pressures in Paros in the seventh century B.C. We have no reason to believe that he ever in any sense reached home. By means of his genius he created from his own life and experience an idiosyncratic version, almost a parody of the heroic legend of *epos*.[2] In his work he was sincere but not incapable of fantasy about himself. The voice which comes to us through the centuries is broken and intermittent but unquestionably individual in the quality of emotions and the attitudes which it insistently expresses.

The nature and content of his poetry make it difficult to separate the poet from the man with any sharpness of focus. Both are independently interesting topics, but they have to be considered together for either of them to be discerned. Perhaps it might be different if more of his work survived, or we had more historical information available about him and his times, but in the chapters which follow the two aspects will be considered in relation to each other. I shall begin by discussing some points concerning his reputation amongst literary men and philosophers in the ancient world. For the moment therefore I shall leave aside such ques-

1

tions as the banning of his books from Sparta,[3] or whether he drove the Lycambids to suicide with his ridicule. I shall be concerned at this point rather to set some less sensational opinions about him into perspective.

His poetry presented difficulties even in the time of Aristotle, who wrote a treatise on the problems (ἀπορήματα) connected with him,[4] together with similar works on two other anger poets, Choerilus and Euripides.

But the span of years in which Archilochus is mentioned by ancient authors stretches from Heraclitus in the sixth century B.C. to the Church Fathers of the sixth century A.D. His fame is illustrated not only by the spread of centuries in which these literary references occur, but also by its frequent and close association with those of Homer and Hesiod.[5] This does not mean that he was thought necessarily to be their equal in every respect, but it suggests that he was classed as one of the great originators who founded the Greek poetic tradition.[6]

Ancient literary criticism, especially in the Archaic and Classical ages of Greece, tends to emphasize the moral and educative value of poetry.[7] The tribute paid by later authors to Archilochus in associating his name with these two great founding fathers reflects literary as well as moral assessment of his work. In the fourth century B.C., Alcidamas, the sophist and rhetorician, notes the paradoxical fact that the people of Paros, Archilochus' native island, honoured his memory in spite of his bad character as a βλάσφημος, a man of bitter and abusive tongue.[8] A monument dedicated to his cult has been discovered in Paros, containing extensive fragments of an inscription by a certain Mnesiepes, and this recalls, with other information, the pious respect in which he was held.[9] It is attributed to the third century B.C.; in the first century B.C. another inscription was set up in the *Archilocheion* which contains portions of a biography of Archilochus by Demeas, a local historian of the island in the fourth century B.C.[10]

However, Archilochus' earliest known critic, the philosopher Heraclitus,[11] placed him beside Homer as an object for disapproval. He suggested that they both ought to be driven off the race-course with cudgels. We may suppose that his principal objection to them was that they were preoccupied with transient *mythos* rather than reliable *logos;* but the fact that he mentions them together implies a recognition of Archilochus' status as a poet. Glaucos of Rhegium, a contemporary of the atomistic philosopher Democritus, seems to have examined Archilochus' poetry in some detail in his book *On the Ancient Poets* and to have assessed its literary characteristics.[12]

Another important early testimony is that of Pindar who shows in his ninth *Olympian Ode* (v. 1.) that he knows of Archilochus' hymn in praise of Heracles.[13] He is also familiar with Archilochus' reputation as a ferocious satirist, for in the second *Pythian Ode* (v. 54 ff) he imagines Archilochus, far off in time, afflicted by poverty, with his mind poisoned and deluded by its propensity to furious slandering, the profitless nature of which he is unable to perceive. Pindar uses this picture of the ancient poet as a piece of self-admonition, so that he himself may avoid being sidetracked by his own resentments into such barren ways. He is quite sure that satirical abuse, i.e. ψόγος, the characteristic activity of Archilochus, would be imprudent business policy for an aristocrat like himself who earned his living from the patronage of rich and powerful men. His actual comments on Archilochus as 'satirical' (ψογερόν) 'fattening on bitter-worded hatreds' (βαρυλόγοις ἔχθεσιν/πιαινόμενον) (vv 55-56) do not tell us that Archilochus is 'fattening' or 'thriving', which would be a common meaning of πιαινόμενον; but rather that his wit is becoming stupidly obese with the delusion that ψόγος is a fruitful poetic occupation.[14] Pindar's view clearly is that nobody will thrive, physically or artistically, from the practise of this poetic genre.

A. von Blumenthal, discussing ancient opinions about Archilochus, suggests that Cratinus, of all the poets of Old Comedy, was most strongly interested in him.[15] Certainly we are indebted to Cratinus for the phrase: Λυκαμβὶς ἀρχή,[16] which seems to refer to the poet's quarrel with his prospective father-in-law, Lycambes, and the latter's arbitrary behaviour. Whatever its interpretation, this reference, together with another that appears to parody a line of Archilochus,[17] would seem to indicate that the poet and the story of his love-affair were well enough known in fifth century B.C. Athens for this allusion to be understood by a large popular audience. Even if we accept Blumenthal's opinion that Aristophanes was less influenced by Archilochus than was Cratinus, we cannot ignore the quotation of Fg 6 D that occurs in his *Peace* vv 1298 ff.[18] Aristophanes uses the poem in which Archilochus unashamedly mentions that he has lost his shield for the purpose of mocking Cleonymus, a political figure not noted for his courage in battle,[19] whose son is made to quote Archilochus' lines in the play as if they were arguments for peace, which, of course, they certainly were not.[20] Aristophanes' quotation also supports the idea that Archilochus' poetry was famous and popular in Athens in the fifth century B.C.

It seems natural that the poets of the Old Comedy, as specialists in ψόγος, should look back with interest to the work of the father of the genre. No doubt their use of Archilochus' poetry increased its popularity, and may indeed have been principally responsible for generating public interest in it. We may conjecture that Cratinus' play the *Archilochoi*[21] focused popular attention upon the ancient poet. Archilochus' iconoclastic attitudes, by an apparent populism, would probably appeal to the radical democratic sentiments of many Athenians in the last decades of the fifth century B.C. His seemingly complete rejection of accepted values and attitudes and his censures upon established persons and ideas could be seen to qualify him as a spokesman for the δῆμος.

Possibly it was in reaction to this that the aristocratic writer and politician Critias singled out Archilochus for severe criticism in a prose-work of unknown title of which a portion is quoted in the text of Aelian.[22] Critias' remarks are an important source for the biography of Archilochus, and they will be considered more closely in the next chapter. Here it need only be mentioned that he objected strongly to the poet's habit of revealing his personality in all its defects, without concealing discreditable facts about his low origins or his distasteful habits. As a good party-man in the old tradition, Critias disliked the fact that Archilochus was capable of being equally severe upon both 'friends' and 'enemies', rather than following the traditional principle of decent men in Greece by doing good to 'friends' and ill to 'foes'.[23] Critias is most severe about the sentiments expressed in Fg 6 D, in which the poet admits the loss of his shield, for he regarded this as a worse disgrace than having a slave mother, being deficient in feelings of solidarity with friends, or indulging in fornication. Like Aristophanes, he simply interprets the poem as a confession of cowardice.

Critias appears mainly as a moral critic of Archilochus, though we may infer an element of aesthetic disgust in his disapproval, since in his view Archilochus' subject matter clearly includes distasteful subjects that should not be mentioned. G. Semerano accepts that there is such an element in Critias' comments,[24] and adroitly supports this view by referring to the distaste which Critias is reported to have felt for the humble examples taken from common trades which Socrates used to illustrate his philosophical arguments.[25] To some extent Critias' attitude foreshadows the criticisms which his cousin Plato makes in the *Republic* of certain passages in Homer which seem to him to be morally unconstructive and liable to promote unsocial emotional states in their hearers.[26] Those parts of epic which show amorality in the gods and emotional instability in heroes are to be removed from the text that is used in Plato's projected city. In support of the idea that there was an undertone of literary evaluation in Critias' remarks, we may note that he admired Anacreon, the friend of his own distinguished ancestors and the poet of the sweetness and joys of life and love[27]—an antithesis to Archilochus in mood and art.

Plato mentions Archilochus twice in his dialogues.[28] Actually, he offers no criticism of him; but one of his brief references associates his name with Homer and Hesiod, thus tacitly accepting his importance in the body of Greek literature. Nevertheless, we could hardly expect Archilochus' poetry to be recommended reading in the educational systems proposed for the societies described in the *Republic* or the *Laws*. Alcidamas' statement about the poet, which has been mentioned, is one of a number of examples in Aristotle's *Rhetoric* (1398 b 10 ff) in support and illustration of the point that genius is often duly honoured in spite of concomitant disadvantages or vices that might appear to render it ineligible for general respect. The Chians honour Homer even though he was a foreigner; the people of Mitylene have great regard for Sappho in spite of her being a woman.

Archilochus' name appears in this distinguished company; and it is quite possible that the Aristotelian context depends closely upon one of Alcidamas' treatises.[29] The passage is concerned with examples for use in rhetorical persuasion. Archilochus' high repute in Paros in spite of being βλάσφημος provides the sharpest paradox of the three, and he is naturally mentioned last. We have some proof of the accuracy of Alcidamas' remarks from the inscriptions connected with the *Archilocheion* in Paros.[30] Although their historical usefulness is sometimes questionable, their hagiographical approach[31] to Archilochus' life seems to reflect precisely the point which Alcidamas makes. Archilochus is represented as a poet under the protection of divine patronage, so that when the exasperated Parians banished him for his sharpness, they were immediately punished with sexual impotence by the god Dionysus.[32] Three varying sources, Critias, Alcidamas, and the Inscription of Mnesiepes, agree about Archilochus' outrageous satire. The significance of their agreement is certainly not diminished by the wide differences in their viewpoints about other matters; Critias was a rationalist, influenced by sophists, and an aristocratic oligarch;[33] Alcidamas was taught by the great Sophist Gorgias, and his rationale seems to have led him to a more liberal viewpoint, especially on the question of slavery, which he held to have no basis in nature;[34] the inscription retains traditional, almost superstitious, notions of the power and divinity of poets.[35]

We have seen that Aristotle was interested in Archilochus.[36] We do not know whether his emphasis in his book of ἀπορήματα was literary and interpretative, or more technical, like the books on Homer and Archilochus written by Heraclides of Pontus[37] in the fourth century B.C. He may have used the poems as source material for his lost essay on the constitution of Paros.[38] At all events, his remarks in *Politics* 1328a might almost be addressed to Critias' criticism that Archilochus was accustomed to attack friends as well as opponents. In this passage, which discusses the effects in different peoples of varied intensities of θυμός: the spirited, aggressive and impassioned aspect of the soul, he refers to a traditional Greek notion that this lively element engenders friendship, just as it is capable of promoting hatred.[39] When a person thinks that his friends undervalue him, or are betraying him in some way, his θυμός is accordingly provoked to anger against them just as it was previously stimulated to affection for them.

Dio of Prusa, the Cynic/Stoic orator and philosopher of the first century A.D.,[40] went further in his sympathy with Archilochus and suggested that his criticisms of other people, beginning as they did with self-criticism, were a positive social benefit. In Dio's time, educated thought had long been permeated by the influence of those remarkable offshoots of Socratic teaching the Cynic and Stoic philosophies, and so his attitude to Archilochus may be more readily accepted. Aristotle's point, however, is a perceptive one, and he illustrates it neatly by a quotation from Archilochus himself: 'In fact your friends are strangling you'.[41] It is still a popular saying that with certain kinds of friends, one has no need of enemies.

Archilochus' poetry aroused keen interest in the poets and scholars of Alexandria. We ultimately owe to their care and curiosity about him the papyrus fragments of his work which have been preserved from the centuries succeeding the great age of Alexandrian scholarship in the third and second centuries B.C. The Roman critic Quintilian (X, 1, 59) records that Archilochus was one of the three iambic poets recognized by Aristarchus as being of first rate importance; the other two were Simonides and Hipponax. The epic poet of the *Argonautica*, Apollonius of Rhodes, wrote a treatise on Archilochus.[42] Callimachus mentioned Archilochus' iambic ferocity, and did not seem to approve of it.[43] Aristophanes of Byzantium (257–180 B.C.) composed commentary notes on his poems;[44] so also did the famous Aristarchus of Samothrace (217–145 B.C.).[45] The work of these outstanding Homeric scholars adds to the view that Archilochus continued to be associated with the great poets of the ancient epic. The essayist on the 'Sublime' (prob. first century B.C.)[46] has a high opinion of Archilochus' talent and expresses it by illustrative allusions rather than by direct appraisal of his poetry:[47] presumably his chosen theme of literary 'sublimity' excludes much of Archilochus' poetry from his direct consideration.[48]

In the first century B.C., Philodemus of Gadara wrote about poetry from the viewpoint of Epicureanism. Many fragments of the works of this sensible, but not especially original writer have been recovered from papyri found in Herculaneum, and the process of elucidating his work still continues. Philodemus does not take the view that the poet should be a moral teacher or exemplar of virtue, and he regards as completely lost the cause of poet in the role of ethical mentor. He is ironical in his account of the victory of sordid 'realism' over Greek 'Classical' taste, and says that should a poet now attempt to depict virtuous rather than disagreeable characters he would be regarded as in some way perverse and vicious himself.[49] The names of Archilochus and Euripides are associated in his comments with the more realistic mode, and he is ready to admit their great merits as poets. In one fragment[50] perhaps he seems a little doubtful about the 'realism' of Archilochus' μιμήσις. He also places Archilochus within the same brackets as Homer.

Quintilian's balanced judgement recognizes on the one hand, the vibrant power of Archilochus' poetry; but against this, he repeats the traditional objections to his preoccupation with the grimmer sides of human experience. He says that in the view of some people Archilochus' defects arise from his choice of subject-matter rather than a failing in native genius.[51] He does not explictly offer this as his own view of the poet, but he does not dissent from it, and it is reasonable to suppose that he accepted it at least in part.

We owe to the early Church Fathers a number of the surviving source references and quotations of Archilochus. They knew the two main elements of the tradition: that he was a talented poet; and that his work was biased towards sinister and morally less edifying subjects. Although it remains uncertain to what extent his work was known to them fully or in detail, it would be prudent to be optimistic rather than otherwise about the breadth of his fame and popularity in patristic times. Mostly he was regarded by the great writers of the Christians as an outstandingly bad example of character and conduct;[52] they have much to say on these topics, but they might almost be supposed from their tone to have been unwillingly fascinated by his wildness. Amongst a number of references to him by Eusebius (third century A.D.) is a quotation which he takes from Oenomaus, the stoic philosopher of the second century A.D.[53] Oenomaus criticizes Apollo's patronage of such a libertine, and Eusebius' purpose in quoting the passage is to illustrate the amoral malignancy of paganism. In the fifth century A.D., Synesius represents a different attitude to the pagan Archilochus,[54] showing sympathy with him, for he himself led a similarly turbulent life. At one point, he quotes Archilochus to illustrate a point of military experience.[55]

Archilochus' fame as a major Greek poet brought him attention in Rome. His work found imitators in Cato, who attacked P. Scipio harshly in the mode of Archilochus but avoided the levity of his exemplar;[56] also in poems of Catullus;[57] and later, in Horace's epodes.[58] Archilochus' outspokenness was harsh by the standards of the Roman native tradition of *satura*, and also by those of the assimilated Menippean satire. A closer parallel to his tone and manner is seen in those traditional customs of Italic folk justice, *occentatio* and *flagitatio*, primitive means of using violent protestation to marshal public opinion against an alleged wrong-doer,[59] which Catullus imitated in poems 8 and 42. Horace acknowledges his own debt to Archilochus, and his study of him in the *Epodes* is so close that it forms an important premise for F. Lasserre's ingenious theory that with the aid of this book of *Epodes*, the fragments of Archilochus' epodes to a considerable degree can be reassembled and placed in sequence.[60]

Archilochus' status as an important poet and as one of the great innovators in Greek literature is firm and undoubted in spite of the fragmentary nature of his surviving works. But even if we possessed less of these than the small quantity which remains, we could not deny the powerful impact which his work, together with its projection of an extraordinary personality, made upon the ancient world. The full tally of ancient references to him is discussed in detail by Blumenthal and Semerano. Both these authors do justice to the strange ambivalence with which his fame was regarded. In discussing his selection of ancient references to Archilochus, my purpose has not been to supersede more minute accounts of the history of his reputation. I have attempted to bring out the implied background views of him as poet rather than teacher that may underlie some of them. Although such views did exist, explaining in large measure his fame throughout antiquity, they could not easily be explicitly stated within the conventions of a society which placed its emphasis upon the moral and educative functions of poetry.

We cannot tell the extent to which his works were available or extant in Byzantine times. No doubt the character of Archilochus' poetry rendered it unsuitable for general use in schools. Ancient society was liberal enough to accept Euripides as a school text, a fact to which we owe the survival of a representative portion of his work, but there is no evidence that a standard edition for wide use was made of Archilochus by the Alexandrians. Euripides ceased with the passage of time to seem revolutionary in his ethics: Archilochus' apparent conflict with accepted values was not mitigated by the centuries. It is encouraging to observe that Archilochus' ferocious and telling image of money being poured into a whore's guts[61] (a palpable mockery of the Danaë story) is alluded to by Niketas Akominatos in the thirteenth century A.D.,[52] but how much of the poetry this distinguished historian had at hand remains a mystery.[63] At all events, it is a reasonable hypothesis that Archilochus' poetry was not in wide circulation—indeed it may only have been known from fragmentary quotations or occurrences in surviving anthologies.[64]

Although he characteristically and distinctly belonged to the seventh century B.C., and though his poetry reflects the disturbances, both in internal and external relations, of certain small islands in this period, he clearly represented in his poems two extreme and persistent pressures upon the lives of the Greek individual citizens: that of social duty and that of competitive self-realization, forces which not only were never fully resolved, but were alive throughout Greek history.[65]

II

HIS LIFE, CHRONOLOGY
AND THE 'BIOGRAPHICAL PROBLEM'

Wide agreement is easily found for the following items in the poet's biography: He was the son of Telesicles, [1] who founded a colony on Paros, and his mother was a slave. He was disappointed in a prospect of marriage with Neoboule, the daughter of Lycambes. Possibly he drove some members of this family to suicide by means of his satires. He engaged in politics and war. He died in battle. He said much about himself and his own life in his poetry. He led a wandering life. At times he may have been a mercenary soldier. He lived in seventh century B.C.

I have already presumed upon some of these; although all of them need discussion and support, and, where possible, demonstration. The purpose of the present chapter is to examine topics which particularly relate to those widely accepted propositions about Archilochus' life and times, and to consider the question of the chronological dates of his life. Others of these themes will be considered later, but the vexed question of 'biographism': whether or not we are justified in thinking that the poetry is possible evidence for a poet's life and his attitudes to living, will also be considered here. In the present climate of criticism, this question needs some ventilation in a discussion of an ancient poet. In considering Archilochus, my views about it are to some degree preempted; for one of the premises of this study is that Archilochus is of interest both as man and poet.

Although most of the points considered in this chapter are addressed to the common end of elucidating the life and times of the poet, they lend themselves conveniently to individual treatment under headings which may serve to keep the various strands of the common theme more separate and clear.

Critias blames Archilochus for speaking very ill of himself:

For if he had not published [he says] such a reputation of himself amongst the Greeks, we would not have learned that he was a son of Enipo who was a slave-woman; or that he left Paros through poverty and lack of means and went to Thasos; or that when he arrived he was hostile to the people who were there, speaking ill impartially of both friends and enemies. Nor would we have known, in addition to these facts, that he was an adulterer, had we not learned it from himself; nor that he was a sex maniac and a rapist; nor (what is even more disgraceful than this), that he threw away his shield. So Archilochus did not prove to be a good witness in his own cause, leaving such a fame and repute behind him.[3]

'I do not accuse Archilochus of these things', Aelian points out, 'but Critias does'.

This passage is part of an unknown prose work of Critias. I am tempted to suppose it part of a rhetorical exercise not unrelated to one of his 'constitutions'.[4] A writer who, deserting their constitution in his ἔμμετροι πολιτεῖαι[5], praised the Spartans for their restraint, might be expected to react in this way to the temperamental extremism of Archilochus. I have remarked that Critias' attitude seems to foreshadow or to resemble his cousin Plato's criticism[6] of extremes of temper on the part of Homeric gods and heros in the monumental 'πολιτεία' which we call the *Republic*.[7] I do not wish either to emphasize or to underestimate Critias' influence on Plato. It is clear that there was some influence,[8] although later Critias came to represent much that Plato distrusted and disliked.[9] It is more prudent to say that Critias in this passage, and Plato in the words which he attributes to his characters in *Republic*, refer in their different ways to certain commonplaces favoured by aristocrats who had learned from the sophists not to be afraid of mildly criticizing amongst themselves the received tradition about gods and heroes. Critias may have preached moderation;[10] but he had the reputation of not matching his actions to his sentiments;[11] and this repute would appear to be well supported by the unscrupulous and self-indulgent way in which he lived.[12]

Critias was a poet himself, and a keen student of earlier poets. Some of his verses in praise of Anacreon have survived,[13] and we may well suppose that they did not stand alone but were part of a series of verse appreciations of early poets.[14] I would not suggest that the original series contained a verse disquisition upon Archilochus; but I would infer that Critias' detailed knowledge of ancient poetry included him. His biographical note seems to have been based upon the poems themselves,[15] and his knowledge of older poetry probably was greater than that of many of his contemporaries. We cannot exclude the possibility that he had biographical information in addition to the poet's own autobiographical frankness in the poems themselves. The tradition mentioned by Alcidamas[16] that Archilochus' repute was high in his native island could possibly have been available to Critias. It is not likely to have been an invention of Alcidamas—leaving aside the physical evidences of Archilochus' cult on Paros that have come to light in this century.

Critias seems to have chosen his topics with the purpose of making a plausible attack upon Archilochus, rather than tracing out a biographical sequence.[17] Critias asserted the importance of νόμος ('law' or 'agreed customary arrangement') as the important basis for civilized life, and tended to discount the claims of φύσις (or 'nature') to be the prime motivation.[18] However he did not regard νόμος as fulfilling its function with complete efficiency, and seems to have been concerned about its weakness.[19] Unlike Antiphon the sophist,[20] whose acute analysis of the relations of νόμος and φύσις lead him to choose φύσις eventually as the most significant factor in human life, he seems to have retained his adherence to νόμος, though it is clear that he was not able to exclude the importunity of φύσις' promptings in his own personal life. As a member of an aristocratic family, Critias was probably well trained in the *Iliadic* values of 'honour'. Archilochus might seem from this point of view to be a prime example of unregenerate φύσις, and his attacks upon the honour-oriented society of Archaic Ionian island-culture could easily represent him as a sympathizer with the democratic ideas that Critias distrusted. The 'honour' culture, or 'shame' culture[21] places importance upon the preservation of a dignified posture in the face of public opinion, rather than upon maintaining the individual's internal sense of moral rectitude.

This long-inherited notion of 'honour', which characterized heroes of epic poetry such as Achilles and Agamemnon, became transmogrified by the sophistry of the later fifth century B.C. into a new version of individual pride. This new conception of the self had little to do with αἰδώς, the traditional self-restraint of the aristocratic way of life, but pointed out the pressures imposed upon individual nature by the constraints of νόμος and revealed the energetic and talented person as held down by the shackles of the law or other normative agreements contrived by the majority of lesser men. Such, approximately, is the situation described in Plato's *Gorgias* and in the 'Thrasymachus' portions of the *Republic*. In

Critias we see a man who wanted to use νόμος to achieve a political dispensation which represented oligarchic rather than individualist interests; but who also chose, where there would be no risk of losing face, to follow the pattern indicated by Antiphon, and indulge the promptings of his nature.[22]

We need hardly emphasize further the contrast between Archilochus, who confessed in his poetry all activities, good and dishonourable alike, and Critias, who, within his own circle, could be guilty of behaviour that Socrates stigmatized as swinish;[23] and who at the same time wrote in praise of moderate and restrained ways of life. Critias' criticism of Archilochus arose from a profound contrast of temperament between himself and the ancient poet in addition to obvious literary and ideological differences. It was anachronistic in Critias to wonder at Archilochus' shamelessness in mentioning that his mother was a slave. To an Athenian of the fifth century B.C. illegitimacy was a much more important matter than it had been in the seventh century. After Pericles' law of 451 B.C. an Athenian could not enjoy the privileges of citizenship unless both parents were Athenian citizens—not even if he were a son of Pericles. Archilochus' birth, part aristocratic and part slave (Critias does not mention the first part), probably carried some disadvantages, but these would be relatively slight in comparison with his status as the acknowledged son of a grandee father.[24] There is no need to palliate the story by attempting to show that the poet's mother Enipo could have been of a distinguished, sacerdotal family, or that Critias' remark arose from a story put about by the Comic dramatists.[25]

Archilochus' financial troubles seemed as striking to Critias as they did to Pindar. Critias uses the words πενία καὶ ἀπορία, 'poverty and lack of means', to describe the state of the poet's affairs. Pindar saw Archilochus as one beset by ἀμηχανία,[26] which can signify lack of financial (as well as other) means.[27] Of course, both ἀπορία and ἀμηχανία have the sense of having no mental or spiritual resources to realize one's wishes or extricate oneself from difficulties or problems: consider the philosophical ἀπορίαι of the earlier, more 'Socratic' dialogues of Plato.[28] However, the words appear to convey nicely the connotation of the English phrase: 'lack of means' when it indicates lack of finances.[29] Both Critias and Pindar seem to think that the poet's ἀπορία was aggravated by his fierce temper, as we can see from the context of Pindar's remarks in *Pythian II* and from Critias' reference to his bad relationships with friends and foes alike when he came to Thasos to mend his fortunes. Possibly Critias is echoing Pindar, or, more likely, they are both alluding to the poet's own expression of his plight.[30] And should we accept that an oracle commanded Archilochus to go to Thasos,[31] this would not invalidate the poet's financial motivation in going there.

We have seen that Aristotle adopts a more reasonable attitude to the poet's trouble with friends and enemies. But it is much harder to dilute the charge of sexual aggressiveness that Critias makes against him, which is amply supported by the evidence of the fragments themselves, even allowing a discount for the poet's own assertiveness and capacity for self-dramatization. If we hesitate to translate Critias' use of ὑβριστής[32] as 'rapist' when it is applied by him to the poet, we can look to the Cologne Papyrus for endorsement of this rendering,[33] since it describes what is virtually Archilochus' ravishment of Neoboule's younger sister. We may note the paradox that a society which permitted frankness about sexual matters in its pottery-painting and in the tradition of its Old Comedy should criticize similar openness in poetry; but neither of these forms of art pretended to represent a profound treatment of sexual relationship in their emotional and ethical contexts.[34] Pottery was silent, and thus less offensive since words had greater power.

Poetry had its traditional educative and ethical role, and it was permitted to speak frank admonitions only within the ritual context of Comedy.[35] Euripides' representation of sexual emotion in the female characters of his tragedies earned him criticism from that outspoken, ribald, but essentially conservative genius of Old Comedy, Aristophanes, who ridiculed his favourite theme of ἐρῶσα γυνή,[36] 'woman in love'. Whatever sacral origins or functions iambus originally had[37] were now largely forgotten or ignored, and iambus was regarded essentially as a medium of verbal outrage which could only be accepted in Comedy. In the fifth century version of the 'honour' code, Archilochus' ridicule of himself and lack of shame about his misdeeds could seem even more distasteful than ψόγος directed against others.

Critias' Spartan preferences, which in themselves could provide him with a sufficient pretext for dislike of Archilochus, are further indicated by his opinion that Archilochus' abandonment of his shield was more dishonourable even than his admission of personal vices.[38] The poem in which this event is recorded will be discussed in more detail later. At this point we can simply recall that the method of fighting implied by it probably did not necessitate at all times the hoplite virtue of standing fast at all costs; it may often have involved quick retreat by sea after a raid.[39] Archilochus certainly did value hoplite tenacity, as he clearly indicates in the fragment where he expresses approval of the bow-legged little captain[40] who stands fast in battle.

Considering Critias' political preferences, his personality as far as we can infer it, the atmosphere of egotistical polemic fed by sophistic techniques in which he and his friends lived, and above all, his lack of historical perspective, it would have been surprising if he had found much to admire in the life and work of Archilochus.

Archilochus was the son of Telesicles and a slave. However, we find that people of such birth could make a considerable success of their lives without being ashamed to admit their origins.[41] Let us repeat that it is not necessary to attribute noble origins to Enipo. There is no reason to suppose that Enipo was a noble captive of war enslaved as a concubine, like Andromache or Eurycleia in the Odyssey; or a casualty of war like Hippolyta; nor yet, as we have mentioned, a member of some priestly family.[42] Nevertheless people in Archilochus' situation were capable of a certain sensitivity about their status. Traces of this attitude may be discerned in Archilochus' poems.[43] There are references to bastardy, which are too brief for detailed interpretation; but the relevant words do occur.[44] More significant, perhaps, is his somewhat nervous assertion of his personal importance and capability in the poem of *Papyrus Ox.* 2310.[45] (Aias' half-brother, Teucer, did not suffer under any marked disadvantages, but it must be said also that his position is represented in literature as secondary to that of Aias.[46] We do not know whether Telesicles had other sons. The oracle mentioned by the Mnesiepes Inscription seems to imply that there were more than one.[47] The fact that the oracle specifically invites Archilochus to go to Thasos,[48] presumably to continue his father's work there, might suggest that there were no others surviving or of age at the time of the invitation, but we cannot be certain. Telesicles had a daughter; but again, we have no information whether or not she was of Enipo.[49]

Archilochus' own name would appear to suggest from its etymology that he was destined to be 'captain of a company'.[50] Any such allusion in the poet's name may simply be an aristocratic assumption of warrior caste; but in a person of his birth-status, it might possibly reflect his father's expectation that this son, who would not necessarily be his main heir, might find a living as a soldier. In the tyrant dynasty of Samos, we find the name Sulasōn[51] presumably given in the hope that he would 'keep the booty' that the family inherited. The Greeks were interested in the significance of personal names. This is clear not only from the etymology of the probably ad hoc inventions of minor personal names in the Epic,[52] but from word-plays upon the names of more important characters like Odysseus, whose name may be thought to connote the bitterness of his experiences.[53]

Archilochus was aware of the etymological significance of names, as his use of names (possibly invented) like Pasiphile ('Everybody's Sweetheart')[54] and Leophilus ('People's Friend') indicates.[55] It would be strange if he were not conscious of the significance of his own. There is no conclusive evidence that Archilochus actually served as a mercenary, although his fame has done service through the centuries as the very type of the wandering *condottiere*. Equally, there is no proof that he did not serve in such a capacity,[56] and his poetry suggests that he was sometimes low enough in funds for the prospect to be attractive.[57] At all events he was no ordinary example of a mercenary but rather the spokesman of this adventuring way of life; also the line of demarcation between the Parian adventurer to the colony on Thasos and an actual mercenary was not necessarily clear or precise either with regard to motives or habits. Archilochus expressed the range of vicissitudes that such a life involved.

When Archilochus declares himself to be at once a servitor of the 'lord of the battle-cry' and also expert in the delightful gift of the Muses,[58] he is not necessarily in the first part of his utterance telling us that he is a mercenary soldier, any more than in the second he is declaring himself a professional poet who earns a living from his verse. He is, however, stating his two most important preoccupations and asserting that they are equally significant elements in the integument of his life.

The 'hagiographical' tradition of the Mnesiepes Inscription suggests that even early in his life he was regarded as an unusual person who was under the patronage of the gods. The oracle of Delphi is said to have told Telesicles that this son was destined for immortality.[59] There is also the story of his meeting with the strange women when he was on his way to sell a cow for his father.[60] He exchanged the cow for the lyre which these disguised Muses offered him, and no sign of the cow was afterwards seen on the island of Paros, though the lyre remained substantial enough. This traditional story has parallels. F. Dornseiff adduced the Biblical story of Saul of Gibea meeting with a group of strange women, and thenceforth being appointed to kingship, as Archilochus was to poetry.[61] It is easy to regard the story of the lyre in exchange for the cow as a latter-day mythopoeia on the part of the θίασος of his worshippers in the *Archilocheion*;[62] but it may have represented an image which the man himself entertained as significant. This kind of symbolical encounter is a credible item in the furniture of any Archaic mind, and some such vision could quite easily have occurred to the poet as part of a 'conversion' to poetry.[63]

The *Archilocheion* seems itself to have been under the protection of Apollo,[64] although other gods were associated with it. If we ask why Apollo should have taken an interest in Archilochus, we may suggest a possible answer to the question by framing a parallel enquiry: Why did the oracle of Apollo single out Socrates for special attention? Chaerephon prompted the oracle's response about Socrates by the implicative nature of the question: 'Is anyone wiser than Socrates?'[65] We may suppose that as in the case of Socrates, so also the reputation of Archilochus was remarkable enough to have brought advance information about him to Delphi.[66] Possibly his family had already some acquaintance with Delphi:

the oracle was communicated to Telesicles while he was on a mission to consult the god on behalf of his fellow citizens.

Also, another god's patronage of Archilochus is suggested in the story that Dionysus punished the Parians for exiling him by the infliction upon them of sexual impotence,[67] and that this disability was not alleviated until they restored the poet to the island. The punishment is not without parallel in antiquity,[68] and possibly this story is an attempt on the part of Archilochus' later devotees to increase the significance of their hero; but it would be excessively sceptical to reject the whole idea that seems to underlie it: namely, that Archilochus was specially favoured by the gods.

It is permissible to conjecture that Archilochus' family had some formal connection with the worship of Apollo. Telesicles' appointment to go on the mission to Delphi may not have been entirely upon secular grounds, but we must recall that Lycambes accompanied him and that there is no trace of a special relationship between him and the god. Indeed, this part of the Mnesiepes Inscription may reflect little more than the historical traces of Delphic propagandist activity of the seventh century B.C.[69] There is also the story that Apollo was angry with Calondas, who killed his poet, and that the oracle ordered him out of the temple,[70] refusing to accept Calondas' explanation that Archilochus had been killed fairly in battle.[71] In the seventh century the oracle of Delphi held strong views about blood-guilt,[72] but perhaps more than this is needed to explain why Archilochus in particular was once more singled out for special consideration. A possible answer is that there was a life-long connection between the poet and Delphi, possibly originating in his family's links with the cult, and probably increasing with the growth of Archilochus' poetic distinction.

Other gods are mentioned in connection with the *Archilocheion*.[73] Of these Demeter has a particular significance as the traditional patroness of the iambic verse form, which may have originated in her worship.[74] The cult of Demeter was strongly maintained on the island of Paros,[75] and Archilochus' interest in the *iambos* may be connected with her festivals.

According to Pausanias' description of a painting by Polygnotus of Thasos, a maiden called Cleoboea introduced the mystery rites of Demeter to Thasos.[76] She came from Paros, and her name is associated with Tellis, who is said to be Archilochus' grandfather.[77] This is a doubtful ascription, and there may be confusion between the name Tellis and Telesicles, of which it might be an abbreviated form. Another suggestion is that Tellis might be the poet's great-grandfather.[78] Whatever the facts underlying this passage of Pausanias, the painter Polygnotus saw the poet's kindred in a context involving Demeter's worship. Further, Tellis (or Telesicles) could be a name appropriate to hereditary association with her rites or τέλη.[79]

These suggestions of priestly association are tantalisingly vague; and lack of evidence precludes anything approaching strong probability, let alone certainty. Yet there remains, encompassing the story of his life, an atmosphere of divine interest, a mysteriousness proper to poets who by acknowledged tradition owe their inspiration to the gods.[80] In the course of history this aspect no doubt was given extra colour by the activities of the θίασος which honoured his memory. Both the tone and the sentiments of his poetry suggest that he believed himself to be a special, marked person. Even if we allow for exaggeration in his expression of his own personality and concede that irony and wishful-thinking influenced him from time to time, or even that on occasion the words that seem to express his own feelings are really attributed to other *dramatis personae* in his verse,[81] he still appears as one who believes himself to be unique and meriting more than the ordinary fate. He seems to have been less sceptical about the gods than about the course of human affairs, but he could hardly be considered as a man of deeply religious temper. He mentions the gods often in his fragments,[82] and always with respect, but he does not show a pious awareness and apprehension of the kind that can fairly be attributed to Hesiod.[83] He was to some extent conscious of his power to hurt by means of his poetry, but it is uncertain to what degree he saw his satirical impetus as a magical, or divine gift. His equation of his poetry with his warlike capacities is suggestive of skill learned and exercised in honour of a god, rather than inspiration, though we need not allow the emphasis of that particular fragment (1 T) to weigh too heavily in relation to other traditions about him. This will be considered in a later chapter which discusses the 'magical' aspects of his satire, and the question of its effects upon Neoboule and her family. Meanwhile the Neoboule affair will be looked at simply as a portion of his life-'history'.

NEOBOULE

Neoboule and her father Lycambes are mentioned a number of times in the fragments.[84] The references are spread through the different genres of his poetry.[85] These facts, taken with the proportion of the number of Lycambid references to the number of personal references to people other than Lycambids which are found in the fragments of his verse,[86] support the view that the Lycambids were important in his life. There is no reason to suppose from the fragments themselves that the references are all concentrated in one narrow band of his lifetime during which he was especially preoccupied with this relationship. We might be tempted to infer that the contrary is marginally more likely in view of the variety and range of poetic forms in which the references occur. There is, however, no means of sustaining this inference in hard terms, since it is impossible to establish a firm chronological relationship between the different types of his poetry. For it cannot be maintained strictly, even if it be reasonable to suppose, that his *Epodes* are substantially later than his *Iambics*, *Elegiacs* or *Tetrameters*, or that he had a predominating preference for a particular type of verse-form at certain periods of his career.

Specific references to the betrothal and its breaking off occur in later authors and not in the fragments themselves.[87] It is in these later sources that the references to the Lycambids' suicides occur. A marriage arrangement may be mentioned in Pap. Ox. 2310[88] and this could refer to the poet and Neoboule; but possibly it could refer to somebody else's marriage. Archilochus writes a bold introduction to an *Epode* in which Lycambes is addressed as 'father', (πάτερ Λυκάμβα ποῖον ἐφρασῶ τόδε, "father Lycambes, what kind of a notion is this you have got?").[89] This may address Lycambes with ironical respect or simply as the father of Neoboule rather than as a prospective father-in-law of the poet.

Archilochus mentions Neoboule with what seems like tender affection in a fragment in which he expresses a wish to touch her hand.[90] Other fragments contain remarks which are extremely hostile, and which probably are also addressed to her.[91] The poem of Pap. Ox. 2310 may represent attempts on his part to prevent the relationship from breaking down as a result of his difficult financial situation and consequent pressure by her parents against the continuance of the engagement.[92]

The Cologne poem describes the seduction by Archilochus of Neoboule's younger sister.[93] No doubt he is expressing a desire for the girl in her own right, but the poem contains enough slanderous aspersion upon Neoboule to suggest that an important motive in him is a determination to attack her and her family. He ridicules Neoboule for being lustful and aged.[94] However, his remarks about her age cannot be used as chronological evidence about his life or love-affairs. Very little time is needed for a lover to feel himself enabled to criticize the girl whom he loved and lost as *passée*; and she may well have been still young when the poem was composed. We can be sure that she was beautiful;[95] but no certain statement can be made about her character and personality, nor can we be sure, in spite of Archilochus' hatred, that she herself agreed with her father's rejection of Archilochus.

Lycambes' grounds for breaking off the prospective alliance could have been political or personal or financial (or a blend of these), rather than the ambivalent status of the suitor as the son of a slave and a grandee. It would be rash to say that his birth was of no importance as a pretext for Lycambes when the poet's prospects began to seem less attractive; but if it had been of crucial importance, the marriage would never have been contemplated at all.[96] Possible kinship of the poet with the Lycambidae can only be conjecture, but with that acknowledgement I would put forward these tentative remarks:

(1) Not improbably, two leading families of Paros could be related by blood or marriage, or both. That the poet's family and that of Lycambes were leading families may be inferred from the joint embassy to Delphi made by Telesicles and Lycambes on behalf of their city.[97]

(2) Archilochus' access to Neoboule's sister as deduced from the Cologne Papyrus is more explicable if we assume some closeness between the families which would enable him to devise her seduction. Whether his account is true or fantastic, it would need, even from the point of the poem alone, to have some element of credibility for those who heard the poem recited.

(3) The same poem mentions Amphimedo, the mother of Neoboule, and describes her as a decent woman, now dead.[98] Archilochus' reference to her presents a contrast to his abusive remarks about Lycambes, her husband. Merkelbach and West suggest the possibility that Amphimedo may have been in favour of the proposed match between Archilochus and Neoboule, and her death may have deprived the project of necessary support.[99] This is more attractive than their other suggested motive for his mentioning her name: that Archilochus hated Lycambes so much that he could not speak of him, which does not seem likely *prima facie* in view of Archilochus' unrestrained eloquence on the subject of Lycambes elsewhere. If Amphimedo is supposed to have been in favour of the marriage, a possible reason for her goodwill towards it could have been her relationship with Archilochus' family.

WAS ARCHILOCHUS MARRIED?

We have no evidence that the poet ever married. J. M. Edmonds suggested that he was married to a woman called Tereina, a former prostitute;[100] but this romantic hypothesis is based upon an ingenious rather than convincing reconstruction of the Sosthenes inscription.

GLAUCOS' MEMORIAL AND ARCHILOCHUS' DATE

An inscription of the seventh century B.C. has been found on Thasos and it says:

'I am the memorial of Glaucos son of Leptines;
it was the sons of Brentes who set me up.'

We can be confident that this refers to Glaucos, son of Leptines, whom Archilochus mentions in his poem 68 D (107 T).[101] It need not be doubted that this is the Glaucos whose name occurs without its patronymic in several other fragments.[102] Archilochus addresses Glaucos in a familiar tone, which may suggest that they were contemporaries who had been together in military adventures. Archilochus criticizes the elaborate Lydian style of life which, he suggests, is excessively favoured by his friend;[103] and this may give us a further indication that he is talking to a youngish man. The important effect of the identification of the Glaucos of the inscription with the Glaucos of the poems is that it establishes Archilochus in the seventh century B.C.[104]

No doubt the Parian colony on Thasos was firmly established at the time when the monument was erected. Archaeological research suggests that the colony was well advanced about the middle of the seventh century B.C.[105] Glaucos' burial can hardly have taken place much earlier than this time. The traditional date for the foundation of the Parian colony by Telesicles is 680 B.C.,[106] which is reasonably in harmony with the archaeological findings.[107] Thus we may cautiously but firmly regard Archilochus as being in adult life about the middle of the seventh century.

ARCHILOCHUS AND THE LELANTINE WAR

Fragment 3 T[108] discusses fighting in Eretria, and it may refer to that extensive but obscure conflict known as the Lelantine War. If this is so, the reference nevertheless adds little precision to the chronology of Archilochus' life. Its information is of a general character:

οὔ τοι πόλλ᾽ ἐπὶ τόξα τανύσσεται οὐδὲ θαμειαὶ
σφενδόναι, εὖτ᾽ ἂν δὴ μῶλον Ἄρης συνάγῃ
ἐν πεδίῳ· ξιφέων δὲ πολύστονον ἔσσεται ἔργον
ταύτης γὰρ κεῖνοι δαίμονές εἰσι μάχης
δεσπόται Εὐβοίης δουρικλυτοί.

Indeed there will be no longer many bows stretched
nor will slings be frequent when Ares brings together
the crush of battle in the plain;

> It will be work for swords, causing much grief; for they
> are experts in that (kind of) battle, the lords of Euboia
> who are famous with their spears.

This occurs in illustration of a passage in Plutarch which describes the war-like quality of the Abantes.[109] It distinctly describes hoplite-warfare but does not imply that the poet himself witnessed the introduction of this style of fighting and the supersession of older methods. Its only arguably positive connection with the Lelantine War is the occurrence of Euboea; and, possibly, the intensity of conflict which it envisages.

Since this war seems to have involved most of Greece, it was worthy of Thucydides' notice as a forerunner of the Peloponnesian War.[110] There has been discussion about the dates of the Lelantine war which was principally between Chalkis and Eretrea, but grew when they were joined by allied states. Probably it stretched in time from the later part of the eighth century B.C. into the first third of the seventh century B.C.[111] Plutarch's statement that Amphidamas of Chalkis fought in it emphasizes the claims of the eighth as against the seventh century.[112] Clearly there is nothing decisive in Archilochus' verses either for the dating of the war or that of his own life. He could be taken to mean fighting that took place in the past, or a possible recrudescence of fighting in the future.[113] If this fighting is part of the continuing Lelantine War, his remarks upon it still do not imply that it overlapped the adult or mature years of his life. W. Donlan puts the matter nicely when he suggests that Archilochus 'has caught a moment in a long war'.[114] We should recognize that this moment, vivid as it may be in feeling, though imprecise in fact, need not have been in the poet's own lifetime or experience. Archilochus had a connoisseur's interest in warfare.

OTHER TRADITIONAL DATES FOR HIS LIFETIME

Cornelius Nepos says that Archilochus lived in the time of the Roman king Tullus Hostilius, who was supposed to have reigned between 672 and 640 B.C.[115] Herodotus, in a characteristic 'aside', mentions Archilochus as contemporary with the famous king of Lydia, Gyges, whose rule is regarded as lasting from 687 to 652 B.C.[116] The overlap between these two reigns provides us with a band of years within the century during which we can be reasonably certain that Archilochus was alive and active. This, to be sure, is a generous interpretation of Herodotus' somewhat vague statement; but his words do not suggest that he is thinking of the poet as being alive only at the end of Gyges' reign rather than during its course. [117] Further, the poem which Archilochus made about Gyges is unlikely to refer to the very beginning of his reign, since he speaks in it of Gyges' achievements as being very distinguished and enviable. [118] Probably the poem does not antedate the time of the king's highest fame, which would probably be after 660 B.C. and his defeat of the Cimmerians. [119] Further, the poem seems to speak of Gyges as if he were still alive: its words purport to issue from the mouth of a down-to-earth character, Charon the carpenter, and it would hardly be consistent with this character for him to deny so vehemently that he was not envious of a *dead* king's wealth and splendour.

Nepos' statement is based upon the work of Apollodorus; another reference originating in Apollodorus, and occurring in Eusebius, places Archilochus' *floruit* in 665 B.C., [120] well within the area of overlap between the statements of Herodotus (if we take that as equalling Gyges' reign), and Nepos (Apollodorus). The 'agreement' of Herodotus and Apollodorus, as far as it goes, is helpful; and it squares well with the evidence of Glaucos' memorial and the archaeological evidence. The *floruit*, if it be taken to represent *aet.* 40, presents problems which will be considered later in this discussion. The 'Gyges' poem, taken with the other materials which we have discussed so far, can suggest that Archilochus was active in his art in the fifties of the seventh century B.C. [121]

THE TROUBLE OF THE MAGNESIANS

The preceding arguments are supported to some extent by the fragment in which Archilochus says 'I weep for the troubles of the Thasians, not for the troubles of the people of Magnesia'. [122] The Magnesians suffered the complete destruction of their city before 652 B.C. and the death of Gyges; [123] it is just possible that this disaster took place before 660 B.C. At all events, it happened before those troubles of Thasos which concern Archilochus and it was famous enough to provide a paradigm of civic woe. The misfortunes of Magnesia may have become a proverb by the time Archilochus composed this verse, [124] but even if this were so, it would be of little help with the problem of Archilochus' chronology, since it is as yet impossible to determine the length of time needed for a catastrophe to become a proverb. The poet may be attempting consciously, and perhaps ironically, to conjure a proverb out of a comparatively recent and well-known event by comparing the obscure, small-scale difficulties of Thasos with the calamity of great magnitude that overtook Magnesia.

His reference to Thasos may mean that the poem was written during the poet's time on the island. [125] He tended to react swiftly and to compose shortly after the event which stimulated his emotions. [126] I believe this swiftness of response to apply especially to these fragments which clearly refer to political happenings, the consequences of which he may be endeavouring to influence in their future course by means of his poems. Not only was he a poet of varied, swift and not easily predictable mind and character; he was also an expert publicist. Whatever its occasion, this fragment does not more than underline that Archilochus was of the mid-seventh century B.C.

THE ECLIPSE

A poem of Archilochus which mentions an eclipse is quoted by Aristotle (its first line only); also by John of Stobae, and it appears in a piece of Oxyrhynchus papyrus. [127] The portions which survive assert the superfluousness of human astonishment at any strange thing that may happen in the world, now that Zeus has seen fit to turn noon-day into night:

Χρημάτων ἄελπτον οὐδέν ἐστιν οὐδ᾽ ἀπώμοτον
οὐδὲ θαυμάσιον, ἐπειδὴ Ζεὺς πατὴρ Ὀλυμπίων
ἐκ μεσημβρίης ἔθηκε νύκτ᾽ ἀποκρύψας φάος
ἡλίῳ λάμποντος·

Nothing at all is unexpected; nothing may be sworn to be impossible, or even astonishing, since Zeus, the father of the Olympians, has concealed the light of the blazing sun and made night out of noon-day.

The poem then proceeds to mention a series of comparable impossibilities, a list of ἀδύνατα, [128] and after this it peters out in fragmentary phrases from the papyrus. The ἀδύνατα and all of these seem at first to be much more helpful to the question of establishing a precise chronology than they in fact prove to be.

The eclipse might possibly be any one of the following, which, according to the records took place: 688 B.C., 661 B.C., 660 B.C. 656 B.C., 647 B.C. [129] We have seen evidence which by cumulative effect rather than precise demonstration tends to place Archilochus' adult life somewhere about the middle portion of the seventh century B.C., and accordingly I omit the eclipse of 711 B.C., and on similar grounds that of 634 B.C. [130]

The difficulty of choosing firmly one of the eclipses to fit the poem exactly is disappointing; for an eclipse is an event which in itself is often precisely datable. Unfortunately we cannot positively identify any of these eclipses with a known biographical fact about Archilochus. There seems to be a reasonable consensus in favour of 647 B.C. Th. von Oppolzer's work remains after many years[131] the most authoratative book on eclipses. He accepts 647 B.C., and his cautious view is followed by Ginzel;[132] also J. K. Fotheringham.[133] Oppolzer calculates that the eclipse of 647 B.C. would have been total within a distance practically equal to that which separates Paros from Thasos. The poem seems to describe a total eclipse; but the eclipse would not have been total at noon in this area. It would have been total at 10:15 a.m. However, ancient authors tend to place eclipses at midday, whether they occurred precisely at that point or not.[134] Also, the earth's rotation is gradually becoming slower and the very slight lengthening of the ephemeris involved could produce an error of some hours in calculating such an ancient eclipse.[135] The calculations of this difference have changed somewhat in recent years and a recalculation would be needed to settle this point conclusively.[136] Need for this and other technical exercises is modified when we recognize that in poetry we have not a scientific report of a phenomenon but a literary statement, which has at least as much to do with emotions as with observed facts.

This point is strongly emphasized by R. R. Newton[137] in refuting Ginzel's objections to the eclipses of 660 B.C. and 656 B.C. as candidates for identification in this poem. He points out that the differences from totality of these eclipses which provide the basis for Ginzel's rejection of them are in their numerical expressions trivial.[138] Newton impartially attributes low estimates of reliability (0.01) to the reports of the eclipses mentioned. His astringent attitude is perhaps a healthy counterbalance to over-optimistic literary and historical speculations. Yet it is obvious that the poet is speaking of some strange and striking actual phenomenon, one that either he saw in person or of which he obtained a vivid idea from somebody else's description. The literary meaning of what he is attempting to express in his poem hinges upon this natural event which in itself, an external phenomenon of the world, interests him as a contravention of the regular order of darkness at night and light by day.

HIS FLORUIT

Eusebius' *floruit* for Archilochus in 665/4 B.C. It is based upon Apollodorus, and Jacoby awakens sympathetic echoes when he remarks that he can see no reason why Apollodorus chose this date![139] We may note that it is approximately in the middle of the period of years upon which Herodotus and Nepos (Apollodorus) seem to agree. The custom of ancient chronography is to put a man's *floruit* at *aet*. 40.[140] If this be applied to Archilochus, however, it is difficult to reconcile the *floruit* with other indications about his lifetime, general and imprecise though they are. If his *floruit* is at 665/4 B.C., then his date of birth would be about 705 B.C. If we accept the tradition that he died in battle, then most probably he died before the age of 60, and this would place his death before 645 B.C.

It is difficult to reconcile this *floruit* with the poem about the eclipse. We cannot disregard these eclipses in discussing the *floruit* even though their independent contribution to our chronological knowledge of the poet's life is very slight. Considering Archilochus' tendency to mention events soon after they happen,[141] it is likely on balance that he is speaking of an event that is fairly recent. The context of the fragment, a person speaking about an immediate concern (a father to his daughter), favours this view. Let us compare the eclipses one by one with the *floruit*: if the eclipse of 661 B.C. is meant, Archilochus, given this *floruit*, was 44 years old at the time;[142] if 660 B.C., then he was 45; if 658 B.C., then 47, and if the eclipse is that of 647 B.C., he was 58 at the time of the eclipse.[143] If the poem refers to Archilochus' betrothal with Neoboule, these options are all improbable on the general rounds that the customary age, both in Classical and Archaic times, for a man to be married was about 30.[144]

We might envisage some less usual time of life for a man's betrothal if some other circumstance, such as an alliance for political purposes, were to influence a family's choice of spouse for a daughter. It is not unreasonable to suppose such an influence in the affair of Archilochus and Neoboule. Since the poet refers with relative frequency to Lycambes and his family,[145] it is reasonable to suppose that the incidents which stimulated such references occurred over a period of the poet's life rather than were centred upon the one event, albeit a traumatic one, of his rejection. However, the stimuli which inspired this poem need not necessarily have been of a nature consistent with the poem itself; it may have been caused by some less personal irritant, such as a minor political conflict that awakened in him memories of his thwarted marital hopes of years before.

But the most reasonable working hypothesis is that which suggests proximity of the poet's reaction in this poem to the event or events which caused it to be composed. Whether the eclipse that it mentions is that of 661 B.C. or 647 B.C., we cannot easily reconcile it with a *floruit* of *aet*. 40 in 665/4 B.C. if the people in the eclipse poem are Lycambids. If these people were not Lycambids, we could then suppose that a natural event, recalled from the past or observed at present, served Archilochus as the basis for some poetic reflections about the mutability of human affairs. The *aet*. 40

floruit in 665/4 would no longer be so difficult. However, reasons for thinking that the Lycambids are involved may be deduced from the introductory remarks which appear in Aristotle's text before the line of the poem which he quotes in *Rhetoric* 1418 b 23-29. He is speaking of the persuasive, rhetorical advantages of an author placing his own sentiments in the mouths of other characters, rather than uttering them in the first person on his own behalf. He says that Isocrates uses this device in his *Philippus* and *Antidosis*, [146] and that Archilochus employs it in his satire, where he represents 'the' father speaking about 'the' daughter in his *iambos:* then comes his quotation of the line 'χρημάτων ἄελπτον'. I have put the definite article 'the' in quotes before father and daughter to reproduce literally its occurrence in the Greek ('τὸν' πατέρα speaking about the daughter; περὶ 'τῆς' θυγατρός). It may well be that the definite article means, as it often can in Greek, the equivalent of a possessive, the grammatical subject or logical subject of the statement being the possessor; and so in this context the 'the' with 'father' could represent Archilochus' father on the one hand, while the 'the' with 'daughter' would mean the daughter belonging to that father; that is, Archilochus' father speaking about Archilochus' sister, possibly about the loss of her husband at sea, [147] a disaster to which Archilochus alludes in his poems. [148]

I am inclined not to take this view because of the words in the introductory passage which refer to 'satire'. Aristotle uses ψέγει as the verb which represents Archilochus' poetic expression at this point, and ἴαμβος for the poem itself. ψέγει means basically 'abuse' but it has the strong secondary meaning 'satire', [149] and obviously it represents the practice of ψόγος. Aristotle had made a special study of Archilochus; [150] and it is not very likely that he would use such words as ψέγει in a loose sense simply to represent Archilochus' poetic composition in general. He would not be likely to use it of Archilochus, the prime exponent of ψόγος [151] if the poem was in fact clearly consolation rather than abuse. Certainly the atmosphere of the piece is not that of *consolatio* such as Archilochus' elegy to Pericles about this same disaster at sea. [152] Aristotle is probably referring to *the* (well-known) father mentioned in Archilochus' poetry, and that father is Lycambes. In his epode, Archilochus addresses him as πάτερ Λυκάμβα (*father* Lycambes). [153] His fatherhood is a significant attribute.

However, the Cologne fragment's description of Archilochus' love affair with Neoboule's sister introduces the interesting possibility that it is she who is 'the daughter' in the poem about the eclipse. Aristotle's purpose in quoting the fragment is to illustrate an author putting his own ideas into the mouth of another character in order to give them more conviction and credibility. If the fragment about the eclipse represents the reaction of an astonished Lycambes, who is attempting to assimilate an unpleasant surprise by means of ἀδύνατα concerning reversals of the natural order, this occasion of his speech could well be the surprising news that Archilochus was the lover of Neoboule's sister. This would be a much more piquant commentary on the love affair than that in the Cologne Papyrus. Also, the element of παρὰ προσδοκίαν involved in it would be characteristic of Archilochus. The poem about Gyges evidently contains such an element. Whatever the occasion, however, and whichever daughter is involved, it is difficult to disbelieve that the fragment about the eclipse refers to the Lycambids.

The puzzle of this *floruit* of 665 B.C. in relation to the poem describing the eclipse cannot be finally solved, but the problem can be escaped by accepting one of the following suppositions:

(a) The poem about the eclipse does not refer to the Lycambids, but to other people (or imaginary people); or

(b) Archilochus composed this poem relatively late in his life using an eclipse (actual, recalled or imaginary) as a literary device in a poem chiefly concerned with ἀδύνατα. [154]

I think that the balance of probability goes against (a) and that (b) is a distinct possibility. But it is opposed by the general picture we have from the fragments and tradition of Archilochus as a fiery, swift-tempered, sensitive man, who reacted rapidly to events and experience. The character and purpose of much of his poetry would suggest much the same, and I consider, on the whole, that this picture we have of him is correct. However, he was also a complex and reflective person, and it would be unjust to suppose that he was incapable of changing his mode of composition or that recollection of emotion had no part to play in his work. The evidence available to us suggests that we should regard the *floruit* as unimportant at present. In the present state of our knowledge, it must be left to one side as an unassimilated figure. Further information, from papyri or elsewhere, may give it a renewed relevance in the future. Archilochus was adult and practising his art about the middle of the seventh century B.C. and he probably died before the age of sixty. Cautious assessment of the evidence allows no more than this. Careful hypothesis will permit us a little more; but we understand more about his art, and his ideas and their quality than we can at present grasp about the dates of his life. This is only an apparent paradox, if we allow that a great poet's words can transcend the native times and places which they sometimes deliberately, sometimes unconsciously, but always, invariably, reflect.

ARCHILOCHUS' TRAVELS

When they are considered from the point of view of space rather than time, Archilochus' fragments give the impression of wide acquaintance with the Mediterranean world of Greek cities. It is hard to define his actual travels. He seems to have lived a wandering life,[155] and to have been well experienced in sea travel and its ways.[156] He knew Thasos intimately and also the adjoining Thracian tribal lands, but we cannot be certain that he personally saw all the places that he mentioned. Complete assurance on the question will probably always elude us, but possibly he knew Siris[157] to the West, also other parts of the Western Greek world, and some parts of Asia Minor and the Cycladic Islands. Possibly he knew Eretria,[158] and the tradition mentions his being in Sparta.[159]

He had an eye for landscape as his description of Siris shows,[160] and also for seascape. This may be simply part of his poetic endowment, but he describes places with the kind of perspective that suggests the sailor's rather than the landsman's eye. In describing Thasos as being like the backbone of an ass, he appears to be looking at land from sea rather than from land itself.[161] The controversial 'Gyrian heights' ("Ακρα Γυρέων) probably are mountains of Tenos, viewed from Paros;[162] the context in which he speaks of them suggests not so much his personal observation of them from the sea, as his use of them as predictors of the weather, and, by extension, as the basis of a military or political image.[163] An inhabitant of a small island is unavoidably influenced by seascape, and this must to some degree modify the view that Archilochus' description has an especially maritime flavour. The idea of movement, of impermanence in any one place is clearly to be read in the fragments.[164] He had the *Odyssey* before him as a paradigm for the role of a wanderer in which he sometimes represents himself, and he was acquainted enough with the *Odyssey* to parody it.[165] Clearly he learned from his travels to comprehend the extent of the Greek world as a cultural continuum, and his use of the word 'Παν-έλληνες' need not be confined as the *Iliad's* Catalogue to the inhabitants of northern Greece.[166] It is applied to the 'scum'[167] of all cities who came to Thasos in order to participate in colonisation and war. We may fairly regard it as including Parians and others who are definitively not northern Greeks.

HIS DEATH

The account of the poet's death is obscured by accretions of story and conjecture. We can discount suggestions such as that of the scholiast to Ovid's *Ibis* that he killed himself, [168] or that personal enemies killed him for his satires of them. More probable is the information that he died in battle at the hands of a Naxian called Calondas, nicknamed the 'Crow'. [169] This would indicate that he died before the age of 60, though it is possible he could have been involved in a battle later in life than this. [170] We have no hard evidence for the age at which he died. His poetry breathes the spirit of youth and energy; but that cannot be called in evidence, since the preservation of a youthful spirit is not infrequent in poets. [171] His philosophizing reflections about death and despair provide no index of his age. Apollo is said to have punished Calondas for killing his protégé, even though the killing was in fair fight. [172] The story is often repreated in antiquity and may have an underlying grain of truth, given Delphi's sensitivity about blood-guilt. [173]

THE BIOGRAPHICAL QUESTION

In this discussion of Archilochus' life and times, his own poetry has been a principal source of information about the events and chronology of his life. Consequently the question arises how far an author's own writings may be used in attempts to reconstruct his biography, either to supplement the lack of reliable external sources of information; or to be a substitute for their absence. It is allied to the question of how far biographical information is of importance at all in the study of a poet. From time to time we have touched upon these questions implicitly—Archilochus' sensitivity to events and his reactions to them have been mentioned as provisionally accepted but not entirely demonstrable characteristics of his mind, deduced from his remaining fragments. His subjectivity and egocentricity have been seen as too obvious to be denied; and it may be suggested that in his case man and poetry are effectively 'one'. [174] If these are reasonable premises about Archilochus it is surely not unreasonable to use his poetry to reconstruct inferentially his life and personality with the aid of external source material. But whoever decides to use the poetry in this way finds himself confronting the so-called 'Biographical Problem'.

Newer criticism of ancient literature (now at last catching up with the 'New Criticism' in English literature) emphasizes the importance of evaluating the work which is itself there before the eye rather than making biographical inferences from its 'evidence' or delving into historical and background questions which too often turn out to be irrelevant to a clear artistic assessment of the works. This approach has been increasingly applied to ancient literature over the last couple of decades; and it has been a fruitful new method, reviving the notion of classical literature as the product of live rather than historical personalities. It has discussed their conscious artistic intentions in the company of their works, and the extent to which they enjoyed a greater or lesser success in achieving these. This analytical study of the literary works themselves, unlike the minute philological study of the text-history and grammar which preceded it, and which it resembles alone in its aim at scientific rigour, makes Classical authors seem more immediate and human. In treating them not so much as equals, but almost as contemporaries, this technique divests them of the dehumanizing awe with which they have been regarded and which has to some degree inhibited literary and artistic comprehension of their merits.

Few who are interested in ancient literature can see this as anything but a good effect. However, another result of this approach has been a tendency to undervalue the importance of studying the historical and personal background of an author and his work, the kind of study which Wilamowitz considered to be of the utmost importance in the overall attempt to understand ancient writers. In considering an author about whom we have considerable information apart from his own works, we may now make the choice whether to study his works by themselves, or with the background material which influenced their composition. We are free to choose, with the more recent school of criticism, not to be particularly to be concerned with historical, social or psychological factors. However, when a poet defines himself as so involved in the experience of his own place and time as Archilochus does, we can hardly achieve a reading of his poetry adequate to the standards of analytical rigour required by these newer literary critics in Classics if we exclude information that is available about his personality and background. We need, in such cases, to know about the man, and often the most eloquent and copious source is his own voice. The decision to include or exclude the 'evidence' from the man himself inevitably involves a prior literary judgement, since, as in the case of Archilochus, there are some poets who seem to be particularly personal and who seem to tell us much about themselves in their poetry.

An elegant, witty polemic against the use of biographical material is the essay 'Me ex versiculis meis parum pudicum' which Professor H. F. Cherniss[175] contributed to a recent collection of essays on the literary, as distinct from the societal and background, study of Latin Lyric and Elegiac poetry. In such a context his advice that we should consider what a poem is in itself rather than how it came to be; 'what it is made into' rather than 'what it is made from' is generally appropriate and useful.[176] However, his case against the use of 'biographical' material is too dependent upon forensic extremes in its examples, and insufficiently appreciative of moderate and sensitive use of 'biographical' and background testimony. He quotes as a typical absurdity of biographism the case of a scholar who unearthed material about the conveyancing of a house belonging to John Milton, and recalls the protracted arguments of classicists about the number of Euripides' wives, or the quarrel of Sophocles with his son Iophon.[177] Absurd these instances may be, if they are regarded as of independent significance and their study as intrinsically important. The small historical fact about Milton's house sale can hardly enlarge our vision of his poetry (or of his personality or methods of work). The question of Euripides' wives or Sophocles' law-suits deserves more regard in that such information may provide us with personal vignettes that can assist our understanding of the plays.[178] The nature of the literature being considered is important: the personal life of Catullus or Propertius is more likely to bear relevantly and interestingly upon the literary character of their work than is that of Manilius.

We could say also that background detail was of interest in considering writers whose work is not 'subjective' or directly expressive of their own feelings or personality, on the simple grounds that if we know more of their environment we may know more of their meaning and intention, and, being more aware of the society to which they were addressing their writings, we may better comprehend the writings themselves. Add to this the naive but needful rider for the pursuit of knowledge in humanities or natural sciences: it is impossible to foresee the future usefulness or applicability of any fact or idea in any field of study. We should be prepared to include rather than restrict information about an author, though we can never on any particular question abrogate the duty of judging the relevance of the information. Cherniss warns us that no matter how detailed our background knowledge of an ancient author's life and society seems to be, we cannot ever know all of it,[179] or indeed enough to apprehend its peculiar atmosphere and feeling.

Against this persuasive point can be set the palpable fact that human knowledge is always limited and almost invariably insufficient for a comprehensive account to be given of any subject. No field of investigation can ever be closed; no search ever completely ends. Nobody can say that we had a sufficient knowledge of the structure of the universe; but if we were to say that certain lines of research into it should be closed in the interests of good sense, since we cannot grasp the object of this research ultimately and thoroughly, we might well be cutting ourselves off from possibility of further learning. For certainly we are not likely ever to know enough about some of the more remote galaxies or their origins and structure, or how the whole (if that is what it is) is what it seems to be. A closer analogy to classics in this respect is that of palaeontology, with similarly imperfect data: if would be bad news for palaeontologists if they were to be inhibited by doctrine from conjuring by hypothesis the whole animal and its possible environment from a fragment or two of bone, and were too afraid of error to speculate.

Literary studies can hardly be considered different in essentials from other forms of investigation; nor (without denying differences between the two) am I convinced that the aesthetic or subjective elements in literature place it in a different category from other subjects. Poetry is part of the world, just as are the stars or chemical elements. Restricting the range of critical analysis to the text itself is likely to obscure rather than enlighten. [180] However, Cherniss makes a point that seems especially applicable to the study of a poet like Archilochus, warning against 'the insidious danger the biographical method has in its assumptions that the essence is merely a combination of accidents, that literature is an automatic by-product of external forces, whence comes its tacit conclusion that no literary work has autonomous significance'. [181] This states in vivid terms a peril which can be avoided only by the use of judgement. The danger is not so overwhelmingly intense that we should avoid its neighbourhood. Just as any man is influenced by certain determining factors in his life, personality and environment, and is also capable in his own view and that of others of acting as an agent who makes up his own mind, so too a poet who is moulded and influenced by his inherited structure, his society and his experience, is not thereby robbed of individuality or the capacity and freedom to create his own poetry. Archilochus lived at a time when a man's life was more public in its involvement with the workings of his society, both in peace and war and in the inevitable contentions of a city-state's factions. His poetry has more marked social and historical dimensions than that of some other poets; the former because of his active, open life and his application of his poetry to its various activities; the second because he happened to live in an historical period of intense energy and activity. Our task is to understand his poetry; we may not do this fully because of its fragmentary nature but we can, however, make some progress even if it is only provisional, and we need every scrap of information to reconstruct him from his 'palaeontological' fragments.

Archilochus is acknowledged to belong to the group of artists whose works transcend the time in which they lived, and for which we have devised the name 'classics'. These works are not timeless in tone and character. Although their importance outlasts their own times, they belong in flavour and temperament to the period in which they were written. If we exclude the individual artist and his life from our view of his poetry, we lose a useful aspect of comprehension; especially if we are studying a poet whose poetry was publically and immediately projected into the ears of his fellow citizens, either by himself or reciters or popular circulation[182] without the indirectness, privacy, and remoteness conferred (or imposed) upon the author by modern methods of publication. To the Parians and Thasians Archilochus' poetry would literally be what Archilochus is saying.

THE AUTOBIOGRAPHICAL PROBLEM

The main aspects of this question, which is continuous with the previous one, have already emerged in our discussion. We have alluded to the possibility that Archilochus occasionally indulged in fantasy about himself and his life, and to the possibility that he may have distorted facts for political or personal motives. Allowance needs to be made on each occasion for such factual distortion, and correcting personal or public propagandist bias is made difficult by the absence of independent information which could be used as a 'control' in assessing his 'statements'. Not only does he tell us what he chooses; this selectivity is modified further by the element of chance which has affected the preservation of certain fragments of his work for posterity. The whole remains concealed from us by its loss, although we are guided on occasion by the remarks of those whom we can safely assume to have had his complete works before them, whose prejudices are often enough sufficiently clear to enable their views of the poet to be adjusted.

The persuasiveness and the power of conviction which emerge even from brief fragments of his poetry, in themselves create problems. The nature of the case allows no escape from such difficulties, and it remains a matter of individual judgement how much of what Archilochus says, or is allowed to say by the faulty transmission of his poems, is to be accepted as sincere self-revelation rather than irony, bombast, satire or propaganda. He is often characterized as completely frank and sincere, shameless indeed, in his exposition of his feelings; but this reputation could be a tribute by the ages to his cleverness in projecting through his poetry the multi-faceted image of himself which he himself has devised. W. B. Yeats' theory of a poet's 'masks' does not apply only to Yeats. Many poets speak without insincerity in different modes and on different levels of feeling and meaning. Ambiguity of intention sometimes represents the truth of a poet's mind, and provides us with the most clear and valid impression of his identity. Yet in spite of these and other difficulties, the portrait presented by the fragments is fairly consistent with that of the authors who mention him. Also there is enough consistency in the fragments themselves to suggest that the lost material was for the most part uniform in tone and sentiment with that which we possess.

III

EPIC AND HEROIC

The emperor Hadrian's epigram[1] says that the Muse, in turning Archilo-
chus towards iambic poetry rather than epic, was granting a request of
Homer, who presumably feared the emergence of too powerful a rival
and successor. According to some ancient opinions, Archilochus could be
classed as 'most Homeric';[2] others held that he was close in talent and
distinction to 'Homer'.[3] Hesiod strongly influenced Archilochus, both in
his attitude and the subjects that he treated,[4] and within the epic tradi-
tion. There was also, if the fragments of the *Margites* are genuinely ancient
or even imitative of an old type of poetry,[5] a precedent for Archilochus'
poetic jesting and abuse more formed and 'literary'[6] in character than a
ritual αἰσχρολογία associated with Demeter's cult.[7] Although Archilo-
chus was well acquainted with the poetic tradition of *epos* (ἔπος),[8] he was
nevertheless a critic of that tradition. Making his own way as a poet, and
shaping his own individual art, he both depended upon and divagated
from his predecessors in the epic. In his attitude to *epos* and his use of it,
he was not simply censorious of the accepted style; nor was he anti-
heroic; nor one who entirely rejected the 'honour' code that in one form or
another has permeated Greek society from the earliest recorded descrip-
tions of its member's behaviour down to the present day.[9] Archilochus
continued and modified the cultural traditions embodied in the epic.

The general familiarity of epic poetry in his time and its pervasion of all
art made it difficult for him not to allude to its characteristic phrases in
contexts not exactly appropriate to their original image, and also, given
his sense of humor, sometimes to make deliberate parody of them. Some
of this was probably the poetic diabolism of the iambicist and wielder of
ψόγος; but we may suspect that sometimes it was simply the result of his

36

profound involvement in epic ideas and language; just as in old fashioned 'Anglo-Saxon' communities, reminiscences of the King James Bible frequently occur in ordinary speech, both appropriately and in circumstances where they are quite out of context.

Epic poetry was in its origins oral and formulaic. [10] It was composed and transmitted by word of mouth, and did not depend upon writing either at the stage when it was being put together, or for its recital, or for its preservation and record. The verses of which it consisted were themselves composed of 'formulae': metrically useful portions of hexameter lines which represented set phrases of ornament, substantive references or actions. These admitted various substitutions and changes of component words within the hexameter's metrical and structural 'envelopes'. [11] Some formulae were of great antiquity, scarcely understood even by those poets and reciters of *epos* who were skilled in the techniques of oral formulaic poetry. [12] During their training poets no doubt acquired a vocabulary of these formulae which provided them with the resources for poetic composition, just as a vocabulary of words and ideas equips a modern author. The possession of a repository of formulae as the result of a 'bardic' training does not exclude poetic creativity, [13] any more than does the mastery of a wide vocabulary of words or skill in poetic diction inhibit poets of later times. These formulae do not entail that the composition of *epos* was extempore, in the sense of being completely spontaneous and *ex nihilo*. A poet may settle his individual treatment of a theme before he recites it in words and phrases not every one of which is individually premeditated, [14] any more than every word that is written in our own time is premeditated as a single item.

Milman Parry's analysis of the *Iliad* and *Odyssey* systematically revealed the formulaic character of these poems. Other *epos*, Hesiod and the Homeric Hymns, contain many formulae of phrases of formulaic affinities, and show that the use of formulae varied from poet to poet, and that formulae could be considerably modified to meet individual needs. [15] Archilochus' dactylic poetry (in his elegies) consists almost entirely of phrases 'formulaic' in character and paralleled in Homer; [16] but this need not suggest that his method of composition was itself 'formulaic' in the manner of the old epic poets who were trained in a specifically 'oral' technique. The 'formulaic' reminiscences which occur in his iambics [17] do not add any support to such a view, since reminiscences are all that they need be. Nor, again, does the tone of his epodic verse, which is noticeably less redolent of formulaic influence, indicate that when he composed it, he was, as D. L. Page suggests, [18] in transition between age-old, oral, 'prealphabetic' methods of composition, and a later way of making poetry, which to some extent required the use of alphabetic writing.

We have very little knowledge about the use of writing in Archilochus' lifetime, beyond a few inscriptions, and it is by no means clear to what extent a poet in his period would have had easily available means of writing down his verses or recording them complete for others to read. [19] Archilochus' phrase, ἀχνυμένη σκυτάλη (in an epodic poem), seems to indicate 'grim news' that is written down;[20] but we do not know precisely what he means by this expression, and have no reason to believe that the lost Alexandrian treatises written about it solved the problem.[21] Even if we knew that Archilochus used writing to assist his composition (e.g. in making notes of images or phrases or mnemonic aids), and if we had evidence that his verse was recorded for posterity in writing during his own life-time, it would still not be easy to attribute to him different methods of composition for the various metrical kinds of his poetry.

Even today, in our most literate and bookish age, many poets still work from orally discovered ideas which they refine before committing them to paper as drafts for further working.[22] The closely studied mosaic of working notes and variant versions of W. B. Yeats,[23] who is our modern parallel to an 'ancient' poet, coexist with the fact that he composed orally, by murmuring his embryo verses over and over to himself;[24] and if this biographical fact were not available, analysis of his prosody shows its dependence upon sound of words uttered rather than the spatial juxtaposition of words on paper.[25]

In Archilochus' time, and for centuries after, poetry was mainly something spoken, recited and sung, rather than read.[26] No proof can be found that poets ignored the technological resource provided by the alphabet, but it is clear that writing did not dominate the process of poetic composition in the Archaic and Classical periods of Greece. Use of writing as merely an aid to memory (after the fashion of Plato's cool assessment of written works [ὑπομνήματα])[27] is a different matter; and we cannot tell to what degree elegiac poets did this. Probably the absence of a cheap and convenient medium for them to write upon may in any case have limited their use of writing.[28] The epic parody, *Batrachomyomachia*, which is at least as early as the Classical period, frankly alludes to poetry written down;[29] this may be an anachronism, but it may on the other hand be in accord with the practice of some poets and reciters of epic in Archaic or Classical times.

We have no fixed points between which we can envisage 'transition' from one technical method of composition to another in Archilochus' career of poetic invention. The custom of elegiac poetry throughout its history demanded a certain respectful observance of epic usage.[30] Earlier elegy is more deeply steeped in epic influence, and Archilochus', perhaps, notably so; but there is a difference between using formulae and

being a poet trained in 'formulaic' techniques in some 'bardic', pre-liter-
ate sense. We note that Quintus Smyrnaeus, a most literary poet, makes
abundant use of formulae in his *Posthomerica*;[31] also that the earliest in-
scriptions in dactylic rhythms, though designed specifically to record by
means of the incised word, yet contain formulae.[32] Consequently, I be-
lieve it safer to regard Archilochus' use of formulaic material in some
poems and his attenuation of that use in others, as dictated more by per-
sonal and artistic considerations than by the methodological background
of training.

Archilochus' specific references to the epic, that is, to Homer,[33] are
mostly purposive and pointed. He criticizes the contemporary version of
'Homeric' *ethos*; but he never abandons Homer; and he does not seem
ultimately to reject Homer's view of the world. He attempts a process of
interpretation in order to relate Homer to the world in which he lives;[34]
for this world, in many of its circumstances of living, if not in its essential
philosophy, seems to differ markedly from that which is represented in
the *Iliad* and *Odyssey*. This interpretative adjustment of epic ideas is not
the main endeavour of his work as a poet. It is one means by which he
works out an intelligible poetic style for expounding and expressing him-
self and his own personal feelings so that by sharing them with his audi-
tors, he may convey his understanding of the world, and perhaps per-
suade them to better customs in politics and in their own personal rela-
tionships. He is a teacher in the Hesiodic tradition, who, by his modifica-
tion of that main stream of cultural information, the *epos*, is obliged to de-
velop an independent art and a personal style, a new fusion between the
poetic inheritance and the hard facts of life in his difficult and turbulent
lifetime.

Archilochus' range of references to *epos* is very wide, since there is
scarcely a fragment of his poetry for which an Homeric parallel of some
kind may not be found. His parody of *epos* is not of that sustained variety
exemplified by the *Batrachomyomachia*, in which the complex apparatus of
epic is made to seem laughable by the substitution of frogs and mice for
heroes. This parody represents an attempt, typical of the genre, to make
the lofty and superb seem less than its pretensions.[35] Aristotle regards
Hegemon of Thasos,[36] in the fifth century B.C., as the originator of this
type of poetic exercise; but epic parody, though less sustained in length,
occurs in Hipponax's satirical poetry of the sixth century B.C. Parody
makes the demand upon both its practitioner and its audience that they
should approach it well acquainted with the target of its attack; since
otherwise its main effect is lost.[38] The parody represented by the Sicilian
mimes and φλύακες[39] does not make so great a demand: a general famili-
arity with the outlines of *epos* would be enough for the joke to be seen, just

as it would be sufficient for an audience in Athens, looking at a tragedy with an epic theme, to know the outline of the story in order to grasp the nature and magnitude of the issue being treated. On the other hand, parody like that of the ἀγών in Aristophanes' *Frogs* necessitates considerable knowledge of the works and style of the contending dramatists, Aeschylus and Euripides.

Archilochus' parody is a means, not an end in itself. He is not aiming at the poetic tradition as a prime target, but seeks to modify contemporary views of the inherited 'Homeric' ethos. However, the poety of epic is attacked more than if his object were simply the reform of his contemporaries' views without reference to the tradition which they misinterpret to support them. His blending of hexameter lines with those of iambic in the various metrical forms of his epodic poems is in itself an expression of his purpose to inject some of the bathos of ordinary factual experience into a grandiose epic ideal which has become more ornamental than truly heroic. If the *Margites* is genuinely 'Homeric': either composed in the same period, or by the same poet or poets as the *Iliad* and *Odyssey*, we can say that 'Homer' himself already in his time saw the dangers of taking the heroic *ethos* with too superficial a seriousness and tried to suggest a balanced view of it by alternating iambics with hexameters, or inserting iambics into hexameter passages of a ridiculous poem about a famous dolt of folk mythology.

When Archilochus invites his Muse (presumably) to sing of Glaucos' hair-style: τὸν κεροπλάστην ἄειδε Γλαῦκον (95 T) there can hardly be any doubt that there is a parodic allusion in this piece of tetrameter to the invocation that begins an epic poem. The ornamental, slightly absurd epithet, κεροπλαστής, and the verb ἄειδε, with its epic connotations of a significant story that is promised, suggest ironical exaggeration when they are applied to Archilochus' friend and contemporary, Glaucos. The target is not so much *epos* itself. This is not so close a parody of the beginning of the *Odyssey* as that composed by Hipponax in which he attacks a certain person's insensate greed.[40] Archilochus' phrase is aimed at Glaucos and it probably reproaches him for his excessively luxurious style of living. In effect, the fragment implies in relation to Glaucos 'How un-heroic can a person contrive to be?' and carries with it the suggestion that he improve his ways and become soldierly and austere, and thus worthier of the genuinely heroic spirit of the *epos*.

In his elegiac fragment, εἰμὶ δ'ἐγὼ θεράπων μὲν 'Ενυαλίοιο ἄνακτος/ καὶ Μουσέων ἐρατὸν δῶρον ἐπιστάμενος (1. T), Archilochus tells of his two principal activities, two strands of equal importance in the fabric of his life: on the one hand he is the servitor or 'squire' (θεράπων) of the lord of battles Enyalios, and equally, he professes skill in poetry, 'the delightful gift of the Muses'. The fragment resembles the phrases of the *Odyssey*

with which Odysseus and Nausikaa⁴¹introduce themselves and this sug-
gests that Archilochus is imitating the epic. In his assertive εἰμὶ δ'ἐγώ, he
engages the authority of princely figures in the epic in order to lend
strength to his assertion of his real work in the world, his genuine iden-
tity. Backed by the solemnity of the phrases he asserts that war and poetry
are the most significant preoccupations in his time and for himself; but his
reference to epic characters simultaneously indicates the distance be-
tween their ways and those of his own contemporary Greece. He puts
forward a claim for consideration as a person who is important, not by his
birth perhaps, like the princes in the *epos*, but by the two principal skills
that he possesses; and in using this epic phrase he may indicate that he
thinks of himself as in some sense having 'heroic' status. Possibly he is
also glancing ironically at himself for having put on this romantic Odys-
sean pose.

Another elegiac fragment, 16 T, may also parody the epic: Συκῆ πετ-
ραίη πολλὰς βόσκουσα κορώνας/ εὐήθης δέκτρια Πασιφίλη.⁴² There
seems to be a reference here to *Odyssey* 12,231: Σκύλλην πετραίην ἤ μοι
φέρε πῆμ' ἑτάροισιν. In 16 T, Archilochus is addressing a whore, or some-
body whom he wishes to represent as such, with the words 'Fig-tree of
the rocks, feeding many crows, Pasiphile, the good-natured hostess of
men'.⁴³ Pasiphile is a significant name, possibly invented for the woman
by Archilochus,⁴⁴ and its meaning is 'loving many' or 'loved by many':
'Everybody's Sweetheart'. The allusion to the *Odyssey's* Skylla of the
rocks 'who brought grief to my comrades', makes it a harsh attack indeed
upon 'Pasiphile', whoever she was.

Fragment 105 T is a tetrameter passage in which Archilochus is found
to be addressing his own soul, encouraging it against present adversity.⁴⁵
In θυμέ, θύμ' ἀμηχάνοισι κήδεσιν κυκώμενε, and its subsequent verses,
these may be a reference to Odysseus' famous exhortation addressed to
his own heart in *Odyssey* 20, 18, reminding it that it has endured even
more shameful troubles than the present one which is affecting it. Pos-
sibly there is nothing more here than a general epic influence, and the
sentiments may be merely a commonplace of poetic philosophizing;⁴⁶ but
the wandering existence of Archilochus which resembled in vicissitudes
that of Odysseus, might suggest that he had Odysseus in mind. The fact
that there is no verbal correspondence between this passage and that of
the *Odyssey* makes this idea hard to establish. If it is accepted, neverthe-
less, that the poet is alluding to the *Odyssey* here, it is reasonable to sup-
pose that his main target is once more himself, rather than the epic, which
he is using as a medium for his self exhortation towards a heroic stance in
face of troubles. We may have here also a piece of ironical self-dramatiza-

tion, a wry sting directed against himself for his pose as an Odyssean wanderer.

Archilochus' most penetrating criticism of Archaic attitudes was misunderstood in ancient times. Yet these lines are very 'Homeric' in their frankness, and not at all anti-heroic. I refer to Fg 8 T:

> Ἀσπίδι μὲν Σαΐων τις ἀγάλλεται, ἣν παρὰ θάμνῳ
> ἔντος ἀμώμητον κάλλιπον οὐκ ἐθέλων·
> αὐτὸς δ'ἐξέφυγον θανάτου τέλος· ἀσπὶς ἐκείνη
> ἐρρέτω· ἐξαῦτις κτήσομαι οὐ κακίω.[47]

> One of the Saioi is delighted with my shield;
> which I left behind in a bush, a faultless
> implement (and I did not intend to do this):
> but I myself escaped death's conclusion; so to
> blazes with the shield: I shall soon get
> one that is no worse.

War was one of the prime occupations of ancient Greece,[48] and so it was not surprising that on the strength of these lines, Archilochus and his poetry were banned from Sparta.[49] Critias regarded the fact that Archilochus chose to utter them as the most disgraceful act in a shameless career, far worse than being μοιχός, λάγνος and ὑβριστής.[50] It was the frankness of the admission that caused him most shock, not the episode itself. The Spartan government of the seventh century B.C. probably can be forgiven for their disapproval of these lines, since they contain nothing likely to shore up Sparta's hard-won εὐνομία.

An actual incident seems to be described in which the poet himself, and no mere *persona*, is involved. There is no implication of conspicuous cowardice on his part in these lines, but simply a description of an unfortunate loss that he suffered in the general collapse of the military operation, which clearly involved landing from the sea for a raid on one of the Thracian tribes that were a constant source of trouble to the inhabitants of Thasos. Neither the country nor the attack were well adapted to conventional hoplite tactics, and the quick retreat possibly may have been caused by attempts on the raiders' part to use these in an unsuitable terrain. Much later, also on difficult terrain, the Athenians and Spartans were to discover the inappropriateness of the hoplite phalanx in Pylos during the Peloponnesian War, and the Athenians were obliged to employ a radically different tactic that brought them eventual success. The jokes in Aristophanes about Archilochus as a ῥιψασπίς show that in fifth century B.C. Athens, no less than in Archaic Sparta two centuries earlier, the act of dropping one's shield in flight from the enemy aroused a disgusted astonishment that went beyond ordinary disapproval or contempt.

Although Archilochus was popular with the Comic poets of Athens in the fifth century B.C. as a distinguished ancestor in the art of ψόγος, the obvious quotable fact about him was that he admitted his cowardice in war.[51] Archilochus' verses seem to imply that he regarded himself as much more valuable than the shield; which, in order to point contrast vividly between himself as a living being and it as a mere implement, he describes with the full strength of its honorific symbolism for his time by applying to it the epic epithet ἀμώμητον, 'blameless'.[52] Life has its value apart from the claims of honour: elsewhere he points out that the dead have no glory, no distinction.[53] He seems to present a view of human affairs that transcends the honour code which the epos and the customs of Archaic Greece upheld. His view has its own standard of individual integrity, a calculated endurance, linked with a determination to survive; and in its individualism it suggests comparison with the Homeric heroes—in this case the kind of hero who, like Odysseus, wanders through troubles and hardships without breaking the integrity of his determination to live on and to reach his home again.

These elegiac verses, with their attitude of acceptance of life's hard facts, resemble in their standpoint other fragments of his in this genre. The view which they express suits the needs of the adventurer to new colonies, or the mercenary (ἐπίκουρος) who goes from war to war in search of a livelihood, and not in pursuit of death with the unprofitable prospect of posthumous glory. Archilochus expresses the outlook of such a man, and does it the more powerfully by his use of language that suggests the epic, for in this way he both follows the generic trend of epic as the medium for describing war, and at the same time conveys an overtone critical of this trend. The more he employs epic phrases and formulae, the more he casts a reflective and critical doubt upon the ethos associated with epic. This poetic mode involves parody of *epos*, but it might also be described as ironical, in that it involves more than one level of meaning, and implies criticism of the basic or 'tenor' assumptions in the poetic tradition.[54] Archilochus uses the phrases and themes which every decent man accepted as integral to poetry at that time; but he uses them not simply because they are inevitable for the purpose of effective communication on warlike topics, but with the additional purpose of turning them in a new direction.

His lines would have earned him some disapprobation if he had written them in iambics; but probably he would have aroused less bitter criticism. He does not hesitate to use iambic, with its aischrologic background, to describe a full range of feelings and experience, and a description of his own 'failure' in it could have seemed more absurd and contemptible than blameworthy. However he chose the elegiac couplet for this confession; and its heroic phrases exacerbated reaction to his statement. I think his purpose was to speak his mind about military tactics and their ethics, and to suggest a standard of behaviour that met the realities of life as he saw it in war and politics. He was not in favour of cowardice; in no respect did he advocate it,[55] and he was most unlike the coward Cleonymus,[56] with whose name and repute Aristophanes associates these lines about the shield. Unlike Anacreon, Horace and others, Archilochus did not suggest the poet's immunity from the duty of bravery in battle.[57] He merely spoke common sense, and his misfortune with contemporaries and posterity alike was that he spoke it too brilliantly.

If there were any doubt that he placed high value upon the hoplite virtue of steadfastness in line of battle, this would easily be dispersed by referring to his fragment which praises the little bow-legged captain who can stand firm in the hoplite line rather than the showy handsome gallant, who presents a superficies of epic valour.[58] He clearly has in mind for the latter image, his friend Glaucos with his well-curled hair. Another fragment stresses the importance of practical help from an ally or auxiliary (mercenary):[59] his emphasis is upon reality as against appearance; he is for sincerity rather than show, both in public and military life and in personal relations. He has a strong notion of the individual's true worth as something different from personal appearance or distinction of birth, and his defence of his own integrity of personality shows more resemblance at times in its outspoken pride to the high egotism of Homeric heroes than does the mock heroism of the people whom he criticises or the customs which he seeks to modify.

Of the epic heroes, Odysseus would appear most obvious as a model for him in his life of varied wandering and misfortune. Certainly there are, as we have seen, palpable references to the *Odyssey* in the fragments; but I would suggest that in some points Archilochus presents interesting parallels to Achilles[60]—a figure whose opposite Archilochus has sometimes been supposed to represent in relation to the idea of honour.[61] Both, however, show an intense personal pride and a sensitive concern for their own feelings. They are delicately susceptible to affronts which injure their honour, and as in the tradition of φιλοτῑμο which persists to the present day in Greek culture, honour has much to do with the control and possession of womenfolk.[62] Both were slighted by being deprived of their women, and both reacted in a similar way, by fierce personal attack upon those who had inflicted the dishonour upon them: Achilles in his fiery and abusive resentment against Agamemnon's confiscation of his mistress Briseis;[63] and Archilochus in his ferocious anger against Lycambes for the loss of the marriage prospect with Neoboule. It seems likely, however, that Neoboule was included by the poet in his hostility towards the Lycambid family.

Both the Iliadic hero and the iambic poet went so far in their indignation at the personal dishonour which they suffered that they ceased to consider the ordinary demands of the societies in which they lived. No feeling of moderation or sense of responsibility to others was permitted to mitigate their savage feelings. In the question of honour, a man could sometimes find himself alone, an individualist, and if necessary, a desperate one, unless, like Thersites, he chose to sit down under public humiliation.[64] In an 'honour' society, many people will choose to submit, or to pretend that no dishonour has been suffered by them, rather than face the searing isolation and danger of seeking revenge.[65] To pursue the issue arising out of a dishonour that one has suffered requires a brave and hardy spirit, and not touchy, vain egotism; for this, like Thersites' arrogance, is soon deflated.

One of the paradoxes of the 'honour' or 'shame' system of ethics is that in order to face up to the challenge of public dishonour or shame, a man needs an inward determination; and in both Achilles and Archilochus, this is certainly present, strongly supported by a persistent sense of the justice of their respective causes. The 'honour' code involves much more than the surface interplay of personal vanities. Agamemnon in the *Iliad* represents such superficiality; but Achilles has much more depth not only of self-esteem, but even of a kind of moral indignation that overrides political and social bounds and loyalties. His anger is not mere selfishness, but is based upon the ethical position that men should be honest in their dealings, and when he finds that Agamemnon is not, he is vastly and destructively angry. Archilochus' fury is founded upon a comparable notion: we do not precisely know the circumstances of the dishonour placed upon him in the breaking off of his match with Neoboule, but it is clear from his fragments[66] that he too wishes for an honourable simplicity in relationships between people, just as he demands rigorous honesty about such matters as personal courage.

It has been said that Archilochus was much more of a traditionalist in his attitude to epic and its attendant cultural tenets and observances than he has often been represented.[67] Technically, stylistically, and in his use of themes, he owes much to his epic predecessors, especially Homer and Hesiod. His modifications of the tradition were aimed at relating it to changing circumstances in Greek society, and he cannot be regarded as basically opposed to it, but can with some credibility be supposed to be engaged in attempts to revitalize it. Sometimes his wit produced parody which used epic as a vehicle, but this was not aimed primarily at *epos* as a target. His personal reactions as he represents them in his poetry show him to have many similarities to the heroic type of personality. In creating such a picture of himself, he was not trying to put on the shrewdness of Odysseus or the simplicity of Achilles to glorify himself, but was sincerely asserting old-fashioned beliefs in honesty, courage and honourable dealing.

IV

THE FATE OF THE LYCAMBIDS

There is a tradition, widespread in the first few centuries of our era, that Archilochus killed Lycambes and his daughters by means of his satires. The motive attributed to him was revenge for his rejection as a suitor of Neoboule. Various versions agree that his words drove the family to suicide, and that their method of self-destruction was hanging. Horace is our earliest authority for this catastrophic event, and he mentions Archilochus' revenge four times,[1] referring obliquely but surely to the means whereby Neoboule made away with herself,[2] and he speaks of Archilochus' words 'hunting' or 'driving' Lycambes.[3] Scholiasts fill out Horace's allusions with detail which clearly is drawn from a general tradition. Ovid shows himself acquainted with the story, including its suicidal aspect; and he speaks of Archilochus' poetic weapons being dyed with 'Lycambean blood'.[4] We cannot use this as indicating that Lycambes was a separate victim apart from his daughters; for the adjective is capable of a general, familial connotation, and the reference is of a vague allusive kind.

Ovid's remarks are supplemented by various scholiastic comments, some of them so imaginatively illogical as to give comfort to sceptics about the whole tradition by their very coexistence with the more frequently occurring elements of the story.[5] Martial echoes Ovid's phrase about 'Lycambean blood'. There are a number of treatments of the theme in the Greek Anthology, most of which concern the pathetic fate of the two daughters[6] who are victims of that species of poetic fury which Horace disclaims in himself,[7] glad though he is to acknowledge his imitation of Archilochus' poetic and metrical forms exclusive of their ferocious contents.

47

The poets of the Anthology who mention the affair include Dio-
skorides, whose poem in which the girls defend their honourable reputa-
tion against Archilochus' slurs is important in discussions of this theme.[8]
Oenomaus finds it strange that Apollo should so enthusiastically give his
patronage to an abusive and disreputable character like Archilochus,
who, amongst other misdeeds, pours ridicule upon women who refuse
him marriage.[9] I take it that Oenomaus plural 'women' is a general ref-
erence to Neoboule rather than an actual plurality, although it remains
possible that the poet courted others.[10] Also, the emperor Julian forbade
priests to read Archilochus.[11] No doubt he feared that the poet's outra-
geous works might injure the repute of the reformed paganism which he
essayed; and he may well have had in mind the avoidance of the kind of
criticism of Archilochus which we find in the philosopher Oenomaus. But
it is clear that he knew Archilochus' works thoroughly, and that they
were available to read in his time.[12] From a fragment of his letters, it is evi-
dent that he believed Archilochus to have spoken falsehoods against Ly-
cambes.[13]

Horace and these others evidently derive support for their remarks
from Archilochus' poetry itself, and not merely from a parallel tradition,
though such no doubt existed. Certainly the Lycambids were important
in Archilochus' life and consciousness: as we have seen, there are com-
paratively numerous references to them even in the scattered fragments
of his work that survive.[14] Even if we allow a certain preference for scan-
dalous material on the part of those who quote and preserve his words on
the subject, this in itself indicates the striking and prominent character of
his references to Lycambes and his family as well as the general currency
of the story.[15]

The Lycambidae were an actual family of Paros, and probably of some
importance in the politics of the island.[16] They are not merely concocted
extrapolations from the poems or simple accretions by a mythopoeic pro-
cess like that which represents Sappho in love with Phaon;[17] or the no-
tion, which had considerable comic possibilities, and was used (indeed
possibly invented) by poets of Athenian comedy, that Archilochus and
Hipponax were both lovers of Sappho.[18] Without discounting the ele-
ment of popular fantasy that no doubt influences the story as we have it, it
is reasonable to believe that we are dealing with a version or versions of
some real events, at least until evidence is forthcoming to disprove this. I
agree with G. W. Bond's view that the onus of proof lies upon those[19]
who reject completely the tradition about the Lycambids. The story fits
well with the references to the Lycambids which survive and, though not
one of these unquestionably refers to the event, it is sufficient that the

fragments refer with criticism, hostility and opprobrium to members of the family. Nor need we be surprised not to find it included in the inscription together with the hagiographically respectable story of the Muses and the cow. If the Cologne fragment is genuine,[20] it contributes important evidence to our attempts at reconstructing the armoury of weapons used against Lycambes and his daughters; for the poem is of such a character that would make it difficult, if it gained popular currency, for a family to continue an honoured and self-respecting life on a small island. Thus there is something to be said in favour of an attempt to look once more at the story; for if it is true, it represents Archilochus' most ruthless achievement and one which is unique in our records of Greek life and experience.

Horace's authority as a self-confessed student of Archilochus and his reputation as a man of acknowledged good sense cannot easily be disregarded. If we had nothing but his allusions to the story together with our present fragments of the poet, we would still be obliged to consider the question seriously. As it is, the tradition which fans out from Horace's time provides still stronger support for it. Evidence for its availability before Horace is much slighter, and nowhere entirely unequivocal. In the fifth century B.C. Cratinus refers to Λυκαμβὶς ἀρχή,[21] which indicates that the poet could expect his audience to know who Lycambes was. This might suggest that they knew, or might be expected to know, something about the bad relationship between Archilochus and Lycambes, knowledge which they would obtain from his poems or a contemporary tradition associated with them and his name. This 'fragment' does not entitle us to infer that the story of the suicides was known in fifth century Athens; but we cannot be sure that it was not.

Critias is said not to have known of it either;[22] otherwise he could hardly have failed to include a mention of the Lycambids amongst his hostile comments on Archilochus. It is possible that the story may be subsumed under one or more of the opprobrious attributes μοιχός, λάγνος, or ὑβριστής which Critias bestows upon him; but if it is, the imprint is too faint for us to discern.[23] We cannot tell whether Critias knew of the Lycambids or not, since he confines his comments about Archilochus' sexual life to these three disobliging words, and from the way in which the passage of his prose runs, it seems probable that he decided not to go into more detail, or did not have any more detail to produce.[24] Critias' chosen 'brief' was to point out that the poet was in the habit of revealing discreditable facts about himself in his poetry. Archilochus' attacks upon the Lycambids would not fall into this category (apart from their possible inclusion in the insults mentioned above), for in his assault upon them Archilochus shows himself to be a terrifyingly effective defender of his own honour; and Critias would not wish to represent him in this role. However, it must be conceded that Critias gives us no reason to believe that he was especially interested in the matter.

If we recall Alcidamas' remark that the Parians honoured Archilochus although he was βλάσφημος, we may be provided with a clue to the source of the tradition about Lycambes and his daughters. Archilochus' memory was revered by the later generations of his countrymen, as is evidenced by the *Archilocheion* and its associated inscriptions. But the inscription[25] tells us that Archilochus was banished by his contemporary Parians for being excessively abusive; it is possible this alludes to attacks upon an important family of the island which had tragic consequences for some of its members.

This does not exclude the possibility that Archilochus' conflict with the Lycambid family had political overtones which are lost beneath the personal emphasis of the tradition associated with Archilochus' subsequent cult. The tendency of Alcidamas' brief comment and the evidence about the poet's temporary banishment from Paros suggest that the Lycambid story, with other details of his life, may be of distinctly Parian origin, and may not have become widely known outside the island in the fifth century B.C. In the fourth century B.C. Alcidamas possibly has heard something of it; and for the third century B.C. a papyrus poem provides our first discernible testimony about the suicides.[26]

We do not know whether Archilochus actually wished to kill Lycambes and his daughters. We do not know what his particular intentions were, but there is no doubt that he gave this family warning that he knew how to hurt those who injured him.[27] He also knew how to wield poetic curses, but the surviving examples of his art in this sphere are probably not directed against Lycambes and his family.[28] The 'Strasbourg' epode, which is generally accepted as being genuinely his work, contains a powerful curse;[29] and if we can accept the idea that there is a close relationship between Horace's *Epodes* and the epodes of Archilochus without committing ourselves entirely to M. Lasserre's interesting theory of a precise correspondence between the two sets of poems,[30] we may observe that curses are not infrequent in Horace's book; perhaps we may also infer a correlative frequency for them in Archilochus' epodes.

One fragment of the poet has been interpreted as referring to the self-destruction of this family: κύψαντες ὕβριν ἀθρόην ἀπέφλυσαν: 'hanging [?] they spewed out all their arrogant pride'.[31] The use of the verb κύπτειν to signify 'hanging' (i.e. by a rope so as to cause death) is authenticated only by a late interpretation[32] which itself may be influenced by the tradition of the Lycambids' suicide. It may be an attempt to read the story of their self-destruction into a text where it has no place; since the verb could more easily mean 'hanging their heads in shame'.[33] The masculine plural of the aorist participle κύψαντες shows that the group to which it refers could have a masculine element in it, since the masculine can be used to designate a group of both genders. If these words refer to the Lycambid daughters, they must also include Lycambes himself. There is no reason to suppose that Archilochus' fragment which echoes the Homeric senti-ment that 'it is not righteous to quarrel with the dead' necessarily indi-cates his unwillingness to gloat over the death of those who had dishon-oured him.[34] Even Achilles abused the dead Hector, and in any case, the context of this fragment is lost and we have no idea of its purpose. However, all that we can properly deduce from the κύψαντες fragment is the likelihood that Archilochus observed, noted (or even perhaps hope-fully anticipated) some effects, deadly or otherwise, of his poetic cam-paign against Lycambes and his family.

I suggest that the traditional story is too strongly established to be laughed off as a piece of mythopeia at folk level, or as an invention of comic poets in Athens, and that probably Lycambes and his daughters did commit suicide. The other point upon which the tradition hinges seems assured: namely that Archilochus attacked them in his verse.[35] Archilochus attacked them; and they, sooner or later afterwards, com-mitted suicide. What is the real connection between these two propo-sitions which the tradition regards as cause and effect?

Let us look first at the theory, supported by the analogy of Irish and Arabic satirists' alleged powers, that it was by some magical operation, some spell, that Archilochus brought his victims to suicide.[36] It would be understandable enough if such a view of his powers prevailed on his native island of Paros in the folk-tradition: it was the centre of his hero-cult, and he seems to have been regarded there as a kind of 'holy man', who had a special relationship with the gods.[37] His bitter tongue earned him exile, as we are told in the inscription; but it was the oracle of the god Apollo that secured his recall,[38] and it was the god Dionysus who inflicted the males of Paros with impotence for having sent him away.[39] This would appear to be a fertile ground for legends of his 'magic' powers as a satirist to take root, but in fact we have no specific account of how this vengeful power was supposed to operate. Its 'mechanics' are quite ob-scure to us, and as far as his own attitude is concerned, we simply have the evidence of his warning verses that told how he could hurt his enemies, and the poetic curses which we have mentioned. Even these may be claims in which he himself wished to believe, rather than confident assertions of his powers; they may be the whistlings in the dark of a man who feels wronged, but who is powerless to obtain his rights; mere fantasies of supernatural ability; the delusions of grandeur with which a loser sought to comfort his isolation and poverty.[40] Or else it is a question of a poet who, as Piccolomini soberly put it in 1883, naturally wishes to increase the influence and power of his profession, and speaks accordingly.[41]

Poetic abusiveness no doubt had its representatives before Archilochus, although we can name no examples. The ceremony of outrageous insult and flyting is perhaps to be seen, in some traces at least, in the Homeric poems. Achilles insults Agamemnon; Agamemnon insults Achilles and Calchas; we hear Paris being heaped with insults, almost in a ritual manner, by Hector: Δύσπαρις, εἶδος ἄριστε, γυναιμανές, ἠπεροπευτά; 'Foul Paris, fairest in form, woman-crazy, talker of nonsense',[42] has the ring of some possible predecessor of Archilochus in the art of poetic abuse; and it also has a repetitive, emphatic character that is not unreminiscent of a magical spell.[43] But there is no indication that any magic was intended, either in Homer, or in Hesiod, with his obsessive abuse of the judges whom he nominates as 'bribe-devouring',[44] nor indeed as far as we can see, in Archilochus.

But the analogy of the powers of Irish and Arabian satirists has been put forward to explain how Archilochus drove his enemy and his two daughters to their death. And so, before we go further, we had better consider this suggestion, confining ourselves to the Irish parallel, which involves a community of substantially Indo-European character, like that of Greece. The common lore from at least the sixteenth century onwards,[45] had it that Irish bards could 'rhyme rats to death'.[46] Little detail is known about this procedure, although the last recorded instance of it relates to the eighteenth century. A poetic 'spell' or satire seems to have been used. The poets of Ireland claimed some human victims also; not merely from their own people, but including a relatively sophisticated Anglo-Irish state official,[47] who nevertheless was no less superstitious than those whom he affected to rule,[48] and no doubt the more susceptible to spells on that account. Even in the twilit time of Gaelic social decline, in the later seventeenth and early eighteenth centuries, poets retained their ability to kill. Eoghan O'Rahilly is supposed to have killed a man with his poetry, though as his editor points out, most of the satire of contemporary Irish poets was little more than 'rhythmical barging';[49] a sad genre which we also see exemplified in David O Bruadair's fierce poem against a bar-maid who would not allow him any more credit; this is a powerful piece of invective, worthy in many ways of Archilochus, and expressing, again like

Archilochus, miserable personal circumstances with indignation rather than shame.[50]

This is the end of a long Irish tradition in which poets were honoured, as they were in Greece,[51] and feared, as they do not seem to have been in Greece. Satire was a more important constituent of poetic activity in Ireland than in Greece, and it was organized into a number of different kinds, appropriate to different purposes.[52] In its very early form, Irish poetic satire had a spell-like character, seeking to inflict wounds by the homoeopathic power of words descriptive of them, and not yet paying much attention to the delineation of personal characteristics or individual vices.

This simple magic by innate power of words themselves was a fearful weapon. Coipre Mac Etain's attack upon the king Brés, which is mentioned in an account of the second battle of Moytura, simply compares his condition to starvation, isolation, loneliness and misery of spirit, and in this way, according to the story, irrecoverably robs him of his vitality and confidence.[53] The story is preserved in a manuscript of the tenth century B.C., but it clearly refers to pre-Christian times. Clearly the bard wished to impose a certain physical condition by his curse, which in its comprehensive exclusion of its victims from the society of men and human comforts of every kind resembles the traditional curse of the Bouzyges[54] which the Athenians ceremonially directed against offenders of their city and its laws. The infliction of shame does not seem to be an emphatic element in the Coipre's intention, although any unfavourable thing said about a king or any other man in a high position in ancient society inevitably brought some shame and dishonour to him.

In later satires an acrid note of personal ridicule and sarcastic comment, comparable to that of Archilochus, becomes the dominant element; but the characteristics of the ancient spell do not entirely disappear, and in the seventeenth century we find Feardocha O Dalaigh with spell-like insistence and comprehensiveness calling down the curses of God, the Virgin, Apostles, Pope, priests, monks, widows and orphans upon the party whom he wishes to assail.[55]

A manuscript of the fourteenth century tells how Athirne and his sons made satires about a beautiful woman called Luaine, because she would not sleep with them; and as a result of their satires her face was blemished and she died of shame.[56] Here we have an interesting link between the earlier type of poetic spell, like that from which Brés suffered, and the later more 'satirical' type which induces shame. Shame, or a quite literal 'loss of face' in the case of Luaine, arose from something quite obvious and simple, a beautiful woman's loss of the beauty which brought her honour in her society. She was not merely disfigured by the three blisters of Reproach, Ill-fame and Shame, represented by their corresponding colours of unjust judgements, black, red and white; she was also degraded and, in spite of their injustice and her innocence, could not survive.

Such are the ways of the 'shame' culture, in which honour is more significant than innocence, and disgrace can drive out and overwhelm consciousness of right. Such was the fate of Lucretia, in Roman tradition, who proved herself innocent by the self-imposed trial of death; and such also, perhaps, were the fates of the daughters of Lycambes. And in both Greek and Irish cultures, underneath the complex mathematics of honour and shame, there persisted the magical superstition of simple souls, like the girl described by Theocritus, attempting by the aid of the wryneck on its wheel, to bring back her lover;[57] or in nineteenth century Ireland, the persistence of a belief that to have a poem, even in fulsome praise, made about one was an unlucky thing and likely to bring death. This attitude is well summed up by a countrywoman whose words are quoted by Douglas Hyde. Talking about the dreadful fate of Mary Hines, a beautiful girl celebrated in the poetry of the nineteenth century Irish poet Anthony Raftery, she said: 'Divil long does a person live who has a poem made on them.'[58]

Greek poetry that is known to us has none of this true primitive magic about it. It has been secularized of magic—even the hymns to the gods have a secular flavour. We cannot deny that there may have been earlier, more magical forms, but they are not available to us.[59] The process of rationalization and the adoption of a laic attitude has already gone a considerable distance in the time of Hesiod, whose *Theogonia* does not reproduce the sacral character of the Asianic poems which were amongst its models.[60] Hesiod wishes to teach and persuade, rather than cast spells, in spite of his characteristic fear of ill omens. His wish, like that of any Greek, is not to offend the gods.

Archilochus' connections with the cults of the gods on Paros and his enjoyment of the special patronage of Apollo did not confer upon him the powers of a wizard; but he had a genius for poetry which he and others regarded as a gift of the gods, and this faculty enabled him to deploy his words most hurtfully. He is far off from the world of Coipre, and from that of Athirne, even though we observe a comparable element of 'shame' culture involved in the case of Luaine.

Outside the legend of Orpheus, whose art had physical 'magic' effects, Greek poets did not wield supernatural power, but left that to the gods whom they served. Assertion of such powers would savour of ὕβρις. Nothing in Archilochus' fragments suggests that he regarded himself as a 'magical' person capable of inflicting injury by his words. This did not prevent him from praying down curses on his enemies in his verses, or asserting his power to hurt: the former is what anyone, poet or not, would do to enemies; the latter is part confidence in his satirical genius, part intense hatred, and part a sense of being unjustly treated. If he killed Lycambes and his daughters, it was by shaming them rather than rhyming them to death like Irish rats.

We know from the observation of other cultures than the Greek that shame can kill, and that death can seem preferable to dragging out an ungrateful existence bereft not merely of all the honourable opinion of one's fellow men,[61] but so degraded that the victim can no longer be regarded or be capable of regarding himself as a member of the community. This state of mind is not 'guilt' in the sense of a consciousness of having done wrong or acted against the ethos of society intentionally. It has nothing to do with the 'guilt' culture of Christianity and modern Western society. It is more comparable to a deep sense of social contamination; of being stained or polluted by the onslaught of evil, vice, or injustice. 'Shame' in this sense is not merely superficial, or imposed from without; it arises irrespective of the justice or otherwise of its causation. Life can become unendurable for those who are shamed, afflicted as they are by a self-hatred that cannot be rationalized away by arguing the essential innocence of the sufferer.[62] It is only in the time of Plato that we find it explicitly argued by his Socrates in the first book of the *Republic* that it is less happy or advantageous to commit injustice than endure it.

The suicide of a person irredeemably shamed may be observed in the case of Iokasta (Epikaste in Homer). Homer's version simply relates that she kills herself for shame,[63] as a result of finding out the nature of her relationship to Oedipus; Sophocles' Iokasta only decides to kill herself when it becomes apparent to her that the incestuous relationship is inevitably going to be published at large.[64] The story of Phaedra and Hippolytus is more complex: in her decision to kill herself and leave a message alleging her dishonour at the hands of Hippolytus, thereby implicating him in the shame which she herself has suffered as a result of his rejection of her love, she certainly utilizes the ethical equipment of the kind of society that emphasizes shame and honour as standards of its members. Whether she also feels 'guilt' in addition to shame, is arguable; but her action can be interpreted in terms of 'shame' or honour, and probably many Athenians of the fifth century who witnessed Euripides' Hippolytus plays simply understood it in that way.

Further, there is evidence that the Greeks feared the dead, especially the spirits of those who had been unjustly killed. J. G. Frazer points out an interesting survival in Greece of a very primitive way of driving such spirits away, when he mentions in the course of his general discussion of fear of the dead in many cultures, the example of Aigisthus in Euripides' *Electra*[65] throwing stones at the tomb of Agamemnon, whom he has murdered. He mentions elsewhere our one piece of evidence for the fear of the spirits of suicides in Greece: a reference in Aeschines to the custom of burying a suicides's hand separate from the corpse—so that the dead man cannot use the hand against others which he has used so mercilessly against himself.[66]

I do not suggest that these points represent the most important part of the Lycambids' motivation in killing themselves; but the idea of suicide as an act of revenge may very well have been familiar enough.[67] By killing themselves, they vanquish the person who has driven them to do the deed; it is he who, being left behind, must justify himself before the world, and their ghosts persist to do him harm amongst his fellow citizens.

The most pressing motive for Lycambes and his daughters to seek their own deaths would hardly be this desire for revenge, but more probably a conviction that for all practical purposes they were already dead because their honour had been killed. It is probable that the process whereby they were brought to the state of mind in which they killed themselves lasted over a period in which, possibly for years, they endured the fury of Archilochus' poetic attacks upon them.[68] Some climax of vexation could be inferred finally to have made life intolerable for them. If this is a reasonable hypothesis, have we in the remains of Archilochus' poetry any fragment which seems to be a suitable candidate for the part of final detonator of the family's misery? Of the number of fragments which have an insulting character and refer to women, there are some that probably do not apply to the Lycambids at all, or at least are in doubt. None of these smaller fragments seems, in the present state of our knowledge, to fit this role. But the power and ferocity, the ingenuity of scurrilous description and sexual allusion in the Cologne fragment strongly favour its claims for this honour. Who, even now, could endure without anguish the singing of such a song against themselves in the streets? It and presumably others like it which are lost could be used as hammer-blows to shatter the position of the Lycambids in their society..

V

BEAUTY AND OBSCENITY

Archilochus is the first poet in our literary tradition to use sexuality in a conscious and deliberate way as a main theme in his poetry,[1] openly discussing the effects of sexual emotion both upon himself and others.[2] He describes the weakness, despair, beauty and sordidness of love. He also has a delicate appreciation of female beauty and sexual attraction. Possibly it was rejection by the Lycambids which stimulated his natural violence of temper and brought into his art its strong flavour of sexual resentment. But we cannot be certain whether his sexual outspokenness was simply peculiar to himself as an individual, an innovation in art which sprang fully and cruelly armed from his own troubled spirit, or whether he was led by his experiences to develop it from the ritual licence associated with Demeter's cult.[3]

We can fairly say that the vehemence of his attack upon the Lycambid family, even if it is judged only by its supposed results, involved much more than the mere projection of an earth-cult's ritual persiflage into the actual daily life of a Parian family. When we look at the fragments which concern them, we see him studying them closely as people, and this scrutiny, combined with the obscenity of his comments,[4] must have become a brutally crushing weapon.

Probably his obscene references were in part a secularization of ritual abuse. The sacral associations of this ψόγος doubtless did not make it any the less powerful in its effects when it was used outside the sphere of religious ceremony. However, he probably did not use words as magic spells, but as poetic cudgels which degraded and unshaped the clearly defined form of his enemies' reputations, just as physical blows might alter the configuration of a beautiful body. This was an aspect of satirical attack well understood by Cicero who saw the public 'image' which he had created of Pompey as a kind of painting upon which he had laboured with the meticulous art of an Apelles,[5] and lamented bitterly at its being blotched and smeared by obscene abuse—the famous 'Archilochean' edicts of the consul Bibulus.

No comprehensive definition of the 'obscene'[6] is available; but as in the case of other psychosocial concepts, there are clear points of reference from which an outline of its nature may be inferred. Nor can we produce a universally acceptable definition of 'humour',[7] but it may readily be acknowledged that humour has some similarity to verbal and visual wit, to satire, logical incongruity, irony, paronomasia, and other ideas which similarly involve an appreciation of different, coexistent levels of meaning in the same situations, utterances or concepts. These items are difficult to describe in philosophical or psychological terms, but their occurrence is usually recognizable, even though this recognition may be affected by varying cultural factors.

The 'obscene' in our culture (and also in its ancestral Greek form) has to do with offence given to the moral or aesthetic sensibilities of those who come into contact with it, and who react with shame and disgust at its occurrence.[8] Within wide variations, it seems to have a core of concern with the aspects of sexuality that in our predominantly dualistic world seem dirty and degrading, the kind of idea represented by William Butler Yeats' words: 'For love has placed his mansion in the place of excrement.'[9] Insult, violence, physical and mental—involving no mere feral indifference to the functions of the body but a deliberate exclusive concentration upon excrement and sex—are usually regarded as obscene. According to these standards, which to a degree were observed by Greek society as they are by ours, Archilochus composed obscenities. Some obscenity may be unintentional, or directed to a purpose that transcends mere physicality without rejecting it;[10] but Archilochus is usually quite deliberate in what he says. In referring to an intercrural wen (φῦμα)[11] in a woman, his purpose is not clinical or scientific, but poetic, aggressive and degrading.[12]

Archilochus' compatriots on Paros seem to have had no doubt that his utterances were intentionally violent and obscene. They exiled him for blasphemia (βλασφημία),[13] an idea close to the meaning of 'obscenity' in our language. As we have seen, Critias' estimate of him amounts to an indictment of his violence and obscenity, and the succeeding generations of critical opinion in Greece either rejected the poet for these characteristics or (very occasionally) saw some philosophy in them.[14]

In Athens of the fifth century B.C. comic poets were inspired by him, and others took pleasure in the subversive aspects of unbridled liberty of speech. Words still possessed magical power in Greece to this extent, that a word seemed always to the Greek mind to be representative of a 'something'.[15] Whether the theory favoured was that they closely cohere in their very nature with reality, or that they 'imitate' it; or whether it was held that they represent reality by virtue of man's arbitrary agreement that they should, words nevertheless were regarded as being about 'something'. This and related questions are discussed in Plato's *Cratylus*,[16] and for a long time this attitude to language as something important in itself and no mere symbolism persisted in its influence upon Greek thought.

It is sometimes maintained now that language is a social medium, a faculty of man as ζῷον πολιτικόν, which is on a comparable level of importance with sex as a binding and operative medium of society, and thus one of the main sources of invention and variation in the life of our species; that it is integral to our life, and not the luxurious evolutionary contingent[17] of a species with hypertrophied brains. This, as it were, 'neo-Cratylean' attitude suggests a continuity of language with life which may illustrate the way in which violent and obscene ridicule has terrible effects upon its targets without being regarded as magical. Certainly it is not hard to see in Archilochus' fragments this sense of immediacy and continuity between language and action, and no doubt his contemporaries saw the danger that his words presented to the social ordering and control of the powerful force of sex and its attendant pattern of customs which were the basis of personal and family honour and security.[18]

In discussing this aspect of Archilochus we are constrained by the scarcity of contemporary and of earlier material which might provide a basis for comparison. The Homeric *epos* is certainly earlier, but it offers little in the way of directly comparative material in its treatment of sexual themes. We shall see, however, that Archilochus made full use of one of its episodes that involves sex, the Διὸς Ἀπάτη.[19] Yet the *epos* as a whole seems to be without any self-conscious or intense notion of sexuality. We might even be tempted to regard its sexual references as innocent, naive, or, to use an adjective applied wrongly (in my opinion), to Archilochus, 'pre-prurient'.[20] Personal views will inevitably influence the interpretation of the epic passages which deal with this theme, but in general it would be reasonable to say that the attitude to sex in the *epos* is not naive, rather that it is balanced. Sex is a cause of deep emotion only when, as in the case of Agamemnon taking Briseis away from Achilles, it impinges upon the province of a man's 'honour';[21] and this attitude is similar to that which appears in Hesiod, and elsewhere.[22] Otherwise in the Homeric *epos* it is treated with a sense of proportion, an aristocratic coolness which seems to regard it as a part of life which has its pleasurable side, and which is not usually a source of danger.[23]

Hera, abetted by Aphrodite, deploys her sexual attractions in order to seduce her husband away from the scene of action, so that her own tactical plan for the war at Troy might prevail.[24] This is a use of sexuality as a means of persuasion, and as an agent which in purpose and effect aims at something ulterior to immediate pleasure. It is not cold-blooded or cynical: there is humour and sensuousness in the Διός Ἀπάτη episode, although its descriptions are restrained in tone and are certainly not anatomical diagrams. The episode of Aphrodite and Ares in the *Odyssey* also has a humourous and lighthearted tone.[25] Hephaistos is cuckolded, certainly; but he catches the lovers by means of his special skill, and the score ultimately is more or less even between the adulterers and the wronged husband.[26] This kind of sexuality is not a major preoccupation; it does not occupy all the emotional and intellectual space available; it is rather an accepted aspect of experience, kept in its place and not allowed to dominate; for where it does, it can cause a war like that celebrated in the *Iliad* and other epics about Troy.

Thetis advises her son, when he is depressed, to go and have a woman in order to divert himself from his misery.[27] On the other hand, Hesiod describes a society which would not think of using sex for such immediate relief or gratification. In his view of life, woman is an evil necessity rather than a source of pleasure,[28] and the more sensuous and agreeable she seems to be, the more dangerous she is to the security of the man and his family. He warns his brother firmly about the perils which an attractive woman represents to a careful farmer.[29] When he uses the epithet πυγο-στόλος of the kind of woman who is really after the man's property (i.e. the barn), he may be thinking of a courtesan type whose drapery fits tightly over her hips in order to attract the gaze of men. It is also possible that he is thinking of the type of fine lady who is interested in elegant clothes and who would not be very useful as a helpmeet.[30]

The theme of the fine lady married to the rough farmer emerges in Aristophanes' *Clouds* which has a humorous description of the resulting culture clash.[31] Some of the κόραι statues can probably be described as πυγοστόλοι; but we have no reason to regard them as the effigies of whores.[32]

Archilochus' point of view is nearer to that of Hesiod than Homer, but he has an intensity of personal feeling which takes him far beyond Hesiod's expression of the Archaic Greek opinion that women were a prime source of trouble as well as a familial necessity. Archilochus represents an acute personalization of the kind of opinion put forward by Hesiod, for it is clear that he suffers from painful conflicting tensions in his strong sexual impulses, the repulsion he feels for the fleshly activities of life which sexual activity involves, his fear and anger at the social disrepute which his courtship brought him, and his poet's refined comprehension of the beauty of women and the charm of love's more delicate emotions.

We can easily assemble a budget of sexual allusions from the fragments of his poetry. Once more, we should bear in mind the possible element of selectivity that may have led to the preservation by later authors of his more startling or cruder phrases; even though Archilochus' general reputation for free utterance in sexual matters can be set against this. Outspoken sexual references are comparatively rare in Greek literature,[33] and probably Archilochus mentioned sex more often and more directly than any other poet, except those of the Old Comedy of Athens, who were substantially protected from criticism on this count by the tradition of ceremonial obscenity associated with the genre in which they composed.

Direct references to sexual organs occur with some frequency in Archilochus: the σάθη,[34] penis, is mentioned at 55 T; 180 T: *Pap Ox* 23 19 (L/B 68, not included in Tarditi's edition); this is a rude word, as is clearly indicated by Antisthenes' choice of the nick-name 'Σάθων' as an insult for his rival Plato.[35] Another word for sexual organ, the more mild expression, αἰδοῖον, is found in 134 T,[36] in a context which may possibly involve animals. In 60 T, ὕσσακοι, vaginae, is a very probable restoration.[37]

At 53 T, ἵνας τε μεδέων ἀπέθρισεν, 'he sliced away the sinews of the genitals', we may have a description of a somewhat butcherly form of emasculation, which possibly refers to an incident of war; but we have no context to help us to interpret this piece of iambic. A comparably uncomfortable image occurs in an epodic fragment, 198 T: ἀλλ' ἀπερρώγασι μύκεω τένοντες, 'the sinews of the penis are broken (have broken)'. If we regard the verb ἀπερρώγασι as an intransitive, and not the equivalent of a passive, then the reference may possibly be to some spontaneous, diseased, breakdown of potency; but precise meaning cannot be extracted with any certainty for lack of a context. It remains possible that both of these fragments describe the abrasive physical effects wrought upon males by intercourse with an excessively lustful woman. Fragment 46 T πάντ' ἄνδρα ἀπεσκόλυπτεν, 'she (presumably) skinned every man', is an expression of this painful phenomenon, and it has been compared to Catullus' insulting use of *glubere* in stigmatizing the sexual monstrousness of his Clodia.[38] This emphasis upon the messy, unromantic side of sexual relationship is also exemplified in fg 180 T;

$$\text{ἡ δέ οἱ σάθη}$$
$$\text{ὄση τ' ὄνου Πριηνέως}$$
$$\text{κήλωνος ἐπλήμυρεν ὀτρυγηφάγου.}$$

> his penis, as big as that
> of a Prienean ass, a
> stallion fed on corn, spurted.

This moist aspect of sexuality is also mentioned in the phrase παρδα-κὸν δ'ἐπείσιον, fg 224 T, which means 'moist penis'; the expression is preserved as an explanatory gloss on the adjective παρδακός which occurs in Aristophanes' *Peace* 1148,[39] used of a 'place'. These two fragments may be informed by some background influence of that ancient equation of moisture with natural agencies of fertility and life which is illustrated by the phrase ὑγρὰ φύσις, 'moist nature'. This is Plutarch's designation for the province over which the god Dionysus exercises particular authority.[40] The notion of the semen being continuous with the marrow in the 'biological' speculation of Classical Greece is a particular example of this general equivalence of moisture with life.[41] Heraclitus also regarded moisture as the generative source of the cosmos.[42] However, the main emphasis of these and others of Archilochus' fragments which directly mention sex, would seem to be upon coarseness and animality. They may indeed be full of vital force, but they are divorced from more gentle and happier images of love, or even from the ordinary bonds of tolerance and cool affection that were characteristic of Greek notions of marriage in the Archaic and Classical periods.

These two fragments (180 T, 224 T) need not be regarded as necessarily directed against the Lycambids. They may be,[43] but they lack contexts to support such attribution decisively. In his references to sex, the poet need not have confined himself to attacks upon the Lycambid family. As a wanderer and casual soldier, he must have been a witness of much random sexuality and probably was a participant in it. In fragments 53 T and 198 T, we may have been vouchsafed the recorded images of pained and brutalized perceptions; matter derived from his experience of war and its aftermath, and then applied to other aspects of life. He must have seen much blood spilled and many bodies mangled as his words in these fragments suggest. His genius, like that of Swift, was both horrified and fascinated by the cruelties of actual life. Nothing but the harsh words of the streets and the army could serve him in his need to express the anguish of experienced and observed reality. Obscenity was the only dialect in which he could find adequate resources for the expression of his feelings.[44]

There is nothing in common here with the sexual primitivism of the *Margites*.[45] An important theme of the *Margites*, as far as we can gather, is that its main character was innocent of sexual knowledge, and shocked by the suggestion put to him by his newly-wedded bride. The type of the stupid, innocent man is a very ancient character in folk lore. He is succeeded by the man who pretends or simulates ignorance and sluggishness of wit. Margites and M. Brutus[46] are contrasting, but not unrepresentative specimens of the types; and the naiveté which Socrates put on as his philosophical persona, probably seemed somewhat familiar as well as weirdly idiosyncratic in the sight of his contemporaries. The μῖμος, with its confrontation of the εἴρων, the apparent simpleton, and the ἀλαζών or braggart,[47] showed that in the sophisticated society of the Greek πόλις the notion of the complete innocent remained sufficiently vital and emotionally charged that it could not be accepted entirely at face value by ordinary men. Similarly, the *Margites*, which was supposed to be a comical poem, involved a certain sniggering, sceptical amusement at the ignorant man's plight. His ignorance of sex was in itself a symbolic reference to the power and significance of sexuality. As a symbol, it effectively drew attention to the real nature of that which it represented, while at the same time it offered some relief and protection from the full strength of the passions associated with the uncovered reality. *Eros* (ἔρως) was always a terrible force, a νόσος that afflicted humanity.

Even the *Margites*, in these terms, could hardly be considered as 'preprurient', but its contrast with Archilochus' directness is obvious. Archilochus also uses sexual symbolism, often, one suspects, consisting of the cant of street corners rather than deliberately ingenious poetic inventions. This kind of symbolism adds point and vigour to its description of the reality, although it also, by its agency as metaphor or simile, holds off grimness and despondency at a tolerable distance, transforming it into something acceptable, laughable, or at least capable of becoming the substance of disenchanted moralizing, which itself is frequently a comfort to the moralizer, and sometimes to his hearers.

The simile in fragment 29 T seems to exude some of this flavour, as it makes its joke about a kind of sexual activity:

ὥσπερ αὐγῷ[48] βρῦτον ἢ Θρῆϊξ ἀνὴρ
ἢ Φρὺξ ἔβρυζε·[49] κύβδα δ' ἦν πονευμένη

> Just as either a Thracian man, or a
> Phrygian sucks up beer with a straw;
> she was toiling away crouched down

I think that the allusion must be to *fellatio*.[50] The image is deliberately coarsened by the allusion to Thracians and Phrygians, rough barbarians with ludicrous drinking habits. We may have here an attack upon Neoboule, attributing to her the act of a prostitute in the most undignified possible circumstances; but possibly these lines may simply be another preserved vignette of the poet's sordid experiences; the sordidness of which his forceful obscenity here and elsewhere seems to indicate some resentment. At times he must have had a sense of injustice at the instability of his life, and the fortunes that kept him from a place of honour in his city. We have no reason to believe that he never in his life had occupied such a place, but there are certainly grounds for the view that he at some stage lost it.[51] It is reasonable to suppose that he felt it shaming that he should be obliged to consort with prostitutes for lack of eligibility to have a wife of his own class; and that like some broken man or poverty-stricken mercenary, he should be forced by his instinctual needs to seek such scenes as those he has described, rather than casually indulge in them for pleasure.

I suggest that here he probably has Neoboule in mind in these verses and that he is imaginatively projecting her into the kind of bordello circumstances that he knew so well. Elsewhere he seems to cast her in the role of prostitute: he calls her δῆμος fg 241 T, 'public', which is self-explanatory, παχεῖα, 'fat one', which was also commonly used for prostitutes, and ἐργάτις, working-girl, which was another designation for prostitutes.[52]

The idea of 'working' with the meaning of working at prostitution, may occur in fg 29 T: πονευμένη 'working, toiling, being busy'. Also fg 63 T (Pap. Ox. 2312), although it is very imperfect in its preservation, yet seems to have references in it to the 'older girl' (Neoboule), to Lycambes, and possibly to the question of the poet's marriage. It may well have πονήσεται in line 6, a restoration acutely suggested by Lasserre.[53] We may conjecture that this fragmentary piece of iambic is the beginning of Archilochus' serious attack upon the family.[54] If πονήσεται is correct, then he may be foreshadowing insults which he later applies more liberally to the girl and her family. In the Cologne Papyrus, as we shall see, Neoboule is stigmatized as being over-sexed, lustful and immoral.[55] This poem also brings together the accusations of being a prostitute and of waning in beauty which appear elsewhere in the fragments. There are our earliest examples of the 'Fis Anus' theme.[56] If this interpretation is on the right lines, Archilochus can be seen in these pieces also as a brilliant and unscrupulous manipulator of street language's obscene metaphor and allusion. His imputations are severe enough in themselves; but couched in the metaphors of the contemporary gutter which he has metamorphosed into vivid satire, their impact must have been of virulent intensity which we can only with difficulty grasp millennia later.

Other obscene allusions occur in the fragments: ἀπαλὸν κέρας, 'soft horn', if authentically Archilocheian, is a vulgar phrase for the male organ, which preserves some of the enigmatic quality of some of Hesiod's kennings.[57] It also may involve a parody by means of its word play on an epic phrase. A comparable piece of riddling symbolism in ἀηδονίς 'nightingale grove', which denotes the female pubes.[58] The comparison of female genitalia with vegetation is not unparalleled, for example, the use of *hortus*, etc., in Latin.[59] In his ridicule of Pasiphile, (fg 16 T), Archilochus compares her to a fig tree. Apart from the possible Homeric parody involved in this fragment, there may also be a reference to the symbolical equation of the fig with the vagina;[60] though we may also admit that on another level figs were for Archilochus a sign of penurious living (87 T). The following fragment of tetrameter aptly restored by F. Lasserre, probably alludes in a satirical fashion to the myth of Danae's impregnation by Zeus in the form of a shower of gold:

πολλάκις χρόνῳ τε μακρῷ συλλεγέντα καὶ πόνῳ[61]
χρήματ᾽ εἰς πόρνης γυναικὸς ἔντερον καταρρεῖ

often money gathered together by long time and labour
is poured down into the gut of a prostitute

This harsh, raw side of Archilochus' poetic expression contrasts with his aptitude for generating impressions of his own sensibility to beauty. Given this, it is natural enough critics should on occasion juxtapose in their conjectural reconstructions fragments which represent the conflicting diversities of his temperament. In the case of fragments 111 T and 112 T their physical juxtaposition in editions, now almost traditional, is deceptively suggestive;[62] the former:

εἰ γὰρ ὥς ἐμοὶ γένοιτο χεῖρα Νεοβούλης θιγεῖν,

Would that I might touch Neouboule's hand[63]

and fg 112 T:

καὶ πεσεῖν δρήστην ἐπ᾽ ἀσκὸν κἀπὶ γαστρὶ γαστέρα
προσβαλεῖν μηρούς τε μηροῖς

and fall forcefully on her body, and press belly
to belly and thighs to thighs[64]

encompass respectively both tenderness and aggressive sensuality; both
elements are characteristic of human sexual love. We should not, of
course, be influenced by the proximity to each other of these fragments in
some editions, which itself implies a bond between them that is closer
than their merely having the same tetrameter rhythm.[65] Yet these two
fragments are useful coordinates in any attempt to analyse the poet's atti-
tude to one of the primary areas of experience. From this point of view it is
irrelevant whether or not they were closely associated in the same poem
or related poems: the important point about them is that they indicate a
mature appreciation and a clear expression of the coexistence in the same
personality of varying feelings about love. Separately, or together, they
evoke a frank and enduring sense of the delight and excitement of love.
There is no obscenity in these examples and no intention to do more than
speak the truth of human feelings.

A similar atmosphere surrounds two fragments, numbered 25 and 26
in Tarditi's edition, which transmit a memorable image of feminine
beauty:

ἔχουσα θαλλὸν μυρσίνης ἐτέρπετο
ῥοδῆς τε καλὸν ἄνθος

she was pleased holding her sprig of myrtle
and the lovely flower of the rose.

ἡ δέ οἱ κόμη
ὤμους κατεσκίαζε καὶ μετάφρενα

and her hair cast shadows on her shoulders
and breast.

T. Bergk suggested that these fragments were consecutive portions of
the same iambic poem, and this is now often accepted.[66] The source of
fg 26 T informs us that it is part of the description of a prostitute;[67] the fact
that there is a reference to the girl in fg 25 T holding a sprig of myrtle and a

rose also suggests a prostitute. These symbols of Aphrodite probably would not be held so boldly by an entirely respectable maiden.[68] Consequently it is not likely that this is a representation of Neoboule unless she is represented in the guise of a prostitute. The source author who quotes 26 T, Synesius, certainly seems to have first hand knowledge of Archilochus' poems. He is explicit that the reference here is to a ἑταίρα.[69] If this is so, then in these lines is a vignette of feminine beauty,[70] with the stillness and chiaroscuro of the shadowy hair,[71] and possibly a smile like that on the face of an Archaic statue. The flowers, innocent in themselves, are symbols of the goddess of love, and they complete the description of amiable feminine receptivity. It would be tempting, but hardly justified for a modern writer, to perceive a tension between the poet's actual description of the girl's beauty and his knowledge of how she gains her living.

Again, fg 60 T (Pap. Ox. 2311) apparently addresses Glaucos, but it also seems to have references to women. It is too fragmentary to be quoted to good purpose in a discussion with a literary emphasis; let it merely be said that references to women seem to be spread through most of the fragment. Again there seems to be a description of the women and their apparel: an example is the probable restoration of the word ἀκάτια, 'slipper', at line 25; there is also description of the effect of their beauty, for Lasserre has convincingly suggested the enjambment of fg 27 T at lines 5 and 6 of the papyrus where the words καὶ στῆθος seem to match

> ἐσμυρισμέναι κόμας
> καὶ στῆθος ὡς ἂν καὶ γέρων ἠράσσατο

> perfumed hair and breast even an old man might
> have fallen in love with.

One girl alone seems to be described at this point, but there may be mention of a plurality of them at line 22 (πάσαις 'all' fem pl), and we may suppose that these two lines refer to a beauty outstanding amongst them all. The mention of a τροφός, 'nurse', (or some kind of duenna perhaps), may lead to the thought that the poet is describing the inmates of a brothel; and the concomitant suggestion that the word ἑταίρα be restored in line 3.[72] Also in line with this view is the suggestion that the word ὕσσακους (vaginas) should be restored at line 8.[73] This mention of vaginae would, if it is correct, provide another example of the close engagement in the poet's imagination of the coarser, physical aspects of sexuality with an aesthesis that responded sensitively to beauty almost in a romantic way.

This sensibility, comprehending both animality and elegance, seems modern in its consciousness. It apparently accepts, not naively, but with full awareness, that these contrasting elements of experience inevitably coexist as part of the condition of human life; they are not exclusive of one another, but there is yet a sense of satirical anger at their coexistence. As he did elsewhere, here also he may well be using this duality for the purpose of his own feud with the family of Lycambes, for we cannot in the last analysis be sure whether he is describing ladies as whores, or representing whores as ladies.

His appreciation of beauty and his capacity for aesthesis are evident; but so also is his satiric aggressiveness, just as the (possible) ὕσσακοι coexist with the delicacy and luxury of perfumed locks, garlands and the like. Like some medieval preacher, he does not merely accept the duality of fleshly fact and the imponderables of honour, love, friendship and the exhilaration of beauty; he points to the contrast between the two worlds. He draws attention to a cruel wen between female thighs (199 T) an indication which so impressed Horace that he imitated it in *Epode* 8, 516; and he observes with scrupulous malice the decline of the flesh with age. Even the bandying about of rustic obscenities at a festival depends for its effects upon the contrast between the basic physical condition of mankind with the romantic and 'metaphysical' pretensions of the species.

Archilochus seems to have been the first poet in the Greek world whom we know to have used deliberately this duality as a poetic motif. The feeling that he entertained about this unsureness, this ambiguity of life, probably was the mainspring of those satirical powers of his which experience and events prompted into action. The insult that he received (or believed himself to have received) from Lycambes, unfortunately for that man and his family, tapped a source of anguish that was already in his nature. Most of his fragments convey his angry longing for sincerity and truth, and his hatred of ambiguities in people. Fg 54 T (Pap. Ox. 2310), which in part at least is interpretable as a poetic epistle to Neoboule,[74] explicitly warns her not to mistrust him; and that he knows how to hurt those who hurt him. He needs the simple unambiguous love and support which he fears he can never have.

The Cologne Papyrus[75] illustrates this blend of diverse elements in Archilochus' poetic personality. It combines a romantic, almost idyllic atmosphere of dalliance between Archilochus and Neoboule's younger sister with harsh and unsympathetic attitudes to sexual relationships. The contrasts which it contains do much to justify the editorial tendency to place in juxtaposition fragments like 111 T and 112 T.

What follows is the text of a fragment of an epode from a papyrus in the Cologne collection, as published by Merkelbach and West[76] whom I intend to follow substantially in most of their restorations, not because I regard their views as conclusive, but because of their relative caution in conjectural reconstructions. I shall provide a version in English which will follow the meaning of the Greek text as closely as possible, given the fragmentary condition of the poem.

πάμπαν ἀπο(ἀνα)σχόμενος· ἴσον δὲ τολμ[

2   εἰ δ' ὦν ἐπείγεαι καί σε θυμὸς ἰθύει[,
ἔστιν ἐν ἡμετέρου ἢ νῦν μέγ' ἱμείρε[ι γάμου

4   καλὴ τέρεινα παρθένος.   δοκέω δέ μι[ν
εἶδος ἄμωμον ἔχειν.   τὴν δὴ σὺ πένθ[

6   τοσαῦτ' ἐφώνει. τὴν δ' ἐγὼ ἀνταμει[βόμην.
"'Αμφιμεδοῦς θύγατερ   ἐσθλῆς τε καὶ [

8   γυναικός, ἣν νῦν γῆ κατ' εὐρώεσσ' ἔ[χει,
τ]έρψιές εἰσι θεῆς   πολλαὶ νέοισιν ἀνδ[ράσιν

10   παρὲξ τὸ θεῖον χρῆμα. τῶν τις ἀρκέσε[ι.
τ]αῦτα δ' ἐφ' ἡσυχίης   εὖτ' ἂν μελανθη[

12   ἐ]γώ τε καὶ σὺ σὺν θεῶι βουλεύσομεν.
π]είσομαι ὥς με κέλεαι.   πολλόν μ' ἐ[

14   θρ]ιγκοῦ δ' ἔνερθε καὶ πυλέων ὑποφ[
μ]ή τι μέγαιρε φίλη·   σχήσω γὰρ ἐς ποη[φόρους

16   κ]ήπους. τὸ δὴ νῦν γνῶθι. Νεοβούλη[ν μὲν ὦν
ἄ]λλος ἀνὴρ ἐχέτω.   αἰαῖ πέπειρα δ.[

18   ἄν]θος δ' ἀπερρύηκε παρθενήϊον
κ]αὶ χάρις ἣ πρὶν ἐπῆν.   κόρον γὰρ οὐ κ[άτεσχέ πω,

20   . .]ης δὲ μέτρ' ἔφηνε μαινόλις γυνή·
ἐς] κόρακας ἄπεχε   μὴ τοῦτο εφ ιταν[

22   δ]πως ἐγὼ γυναῖκα τ[ο]ιαύτην ἔχων
γεί]τοσι χάρμ' ἔσομαι·   πολλὸν σὲ βούλο[μαι πάρος.

24   σὺ] μὲν γὰρ οὔτ' ἄπιστος οὔτε διπλόη,
ἡ δ]ὲ μάλ' ὀξυτέρη·   πολλοὺς δὲ ποιεῖτα[ι φίλους.

26   δέ]δοιχ' ὅπως μὴ τυφλὰ κἀλιτήμερα
σπ]ουδῆι ἐπειγόμενος   τὼς ὥσπερ ἡ κ[ύων τέκω.

28   τοσ]αῦτ' ἐφώνεον. παρθένον δ' ἐν ἄνθε[σιν
τηλ]εθάεσσι λαβὼν   ἔκλινα. μαλθακῆι δ[έ μιν

30   χλαί]νηι καλύψας, αὐχέν' ἀγκάλησ' ἔχω[ν,
. . .]ματι παυ[σ]αμένην   τὼς ὥστε νέβρ[ον

32 μαζ]ῶν τε χερσὶν ἠπίως ἐφηψάμην

   . . .] . ἔφηνε νέον   ἥβης ἐπήλυσιν χρόᾳ[.

34 ἅπαν τ]ε σῶμα καλὸν ἀμφαφώμενος

   . . . .]ὸν ἀφῆκα μένος,   ξανθῆς ἐπιψαύ[ων τριχός.

The girl speaks:[77]
   "holding off (abstaining) dare (or you dare?) [to desire]
   an equal (love?)[78]
2 if your spirit[79] drives you on towards that which you desire
   there is a girl in our house who now greatly wants [to be married]
4 a fair tender maiden; I think that her
   beauty is faultless; you cause her grief."[80]
Archilochus now speaks:
6 "This was what she said; and I made her due answer
   Daughter of Ampimedo, who was a decent woman and
8 whom the moist earth now covers;
   there are many pleasures from the goddess for young men
10 apart from the divine act itself,[81] and one of these is sufficient:
   those then in silence until (the sky?) darkens[82]
12 you and I shall debate with the help of god;[83]
   I shall do as you ask me:[84] (love urges) me greatly;
14 Do not grudge me, my dear, a quiet entrance in beneath
   your doorpost and your gateway; for I shall thus reach
16 grassy gardens.[85] But now be quite assured: some other man is wel-
come to
   marry Neoboule; I'm afraid she's overdone;
18 her maiden flower has fallen away
   also the grace which she once had. She could never get enough sex:
20 the crazy woman has given proof of the lengths to which she will go.
   Send her to blazes: (let no friend tell me)[86]
22 to have a wife like that,
   and be a laughing stock to my neighbours: I much prefer you,
24 for you are not faithless and tricky:
   she's far too sharp, and knows too many people.[87]
26 I'm afraid that kind of haste would lead me to produce
   blind monsters, like the bitch in the proverb."[88]
28 That was what I said, and I took and leaned the girl back
   amongst the flowers that were in full bloom;[89] in my soft cloak
30 I covered her up, my arms about her neck,
   and like a fawn she stood quite still with panic.
32 Gently I fondled (her breasts)[90] and she revealed her young flesh
   the charm of her womanhood.[91]

34 I stroked her fair body and shot forth the white power [of my seed]
and stroked [the hair] (pubic hair?) of the (golden haired) girl.

At places the talk between Archilochus and the girl seems to have a
pastoral simplicity, as if it were merely the object of the man to gain love
and pleasure, and that of the girl to put up a show of conventional resis-
tance for a while. But the ulterior motive of Archilochus, much more im-
portant than the business in hand, is his wish to attack and injure Neo-
boule and all who belong to her, including this girl. The vendetta[92] seems
to emerge only contingently from the persuasive remarks of the poet to
the girl, but it is really the essential core of the poem, overwhelming and
poisoning its 'eclogic' flavour. The image of the flower, withered in the
case of Neoboule, blooming in the case of those flowers into which the
lover pushes her young sister, links the two women, and they and their
family are both dishonoured in the action described by the poem and in
the very act of description which constitutes the poem itself. The poet in
the role of an outsider and marauder uses the common metaphors of
doors and gates to describe the female pudenda from which he is ex-
cluded, as well as the other familiar metaphors of grass and foliage. As in
Pap. Ox. 2310, (fg 54 T) he sees himself as an outcast; he is denied access
and acceptance, and he howls obscenities at the gates in the sinister
παρακλαυσίθυρον.

An interesting aspect of the poem is that he evidently represents him-
self as refraining from complete intercourse with the girl. The act that he
commits upon her involves the emission of semen, and it has been sug-
gested that coitus interruptus is described. More probably some kind of
masturbation or *frottation* is indicated by the poet's words, which he has
deliberately left imprecise and which in addition are somewhat obscured
by the broken nature of the poem's transmission.[93] Assuming that com-
plete sexual intercourse is not described, it is difficult to suggest the poet's
motive for refraining from it, and contenting himself with a more limited
contact with the girl's body. A mere possibility could be that it was his in-
tention to degrade rather than possess her; and that he was relatively
sparing of her because his main target was Neoboule. Complete posses-
sion of the younger girl would have shifted the poem's centre of gravity.
In spite of his curt dismissal of Neoboule in the poem, the theme remains
that of Neoboule, and the girl of the poem remains a cipher, a shadow of
her elder sister, important only because of her connection with Neoboule.
Possibly he feared that if he should represent himself as possessing her,
he would himself seem once more possessed by the Lycambids, instead
of appearing before his audience as a fierce, avenging alastor.

Only a similar stroke of fortune to that which brought about the recovery of this fragment can tell us more of the poet's background and motives at this stage of his relationship with the Lycambid family. What is clear, however, is that the poem is a powerful instrument of revenge which can hardly have failed to devastate its targets. It has strong epic influences evident in its vocabulary and style: in particular it seems to have much in common with the scene of the *Iliad* in which Hera woos and seduces Zeus. Accepting the satirical nature of the poem, we can suggest that the epic allusions themselves may well have a parodic intention, designed to add to the effect of the whole by alluding to the cool and detached sexuality of the Homeric gods, a balance and deliberation which the poet as narrator seems to wish to arrogate to himself in his role as narrator.

The poem reproduces the somewhat informal and disjointed character of conversation, and does so very skilfully by means of enjambments of sentences and clauses within the pattern of the verse scheme. This lack of evenness is reproduced with considerable polish; for it conveys not only conversation itself, but conversation subsequently recalled and narrated. We can imagine the poet as narrator entertaining his male associates with this account of his prowess.[94] There is no need to doubt that some such scene as he describes took place. Common sense, however, might suggest that he adjusted some of the details in his own favour. He may not have achieved in fact as much as he says in his attempt to seduce the girl. Nor must we forget that in addition to his desire to hurt his enemies, he was probably seeking to engage sympathy from that unknown audience in his own heart, the addressee of many poets' expression of their deepest feelings.

In Archilochus we have no innocence, no 'pre-prurience'. He was consciously aware of the power of *eros*, and he saw the intersection of sexual themes with other strands in the texture of life. His use of images and ideas which pointed out the painful and repulsive aspects of sexual activity was deliberate, and many of his fragments by standards of his own time and ours deserve to be called obscene. This obscenity was not casual. It was integral to his vision of a world composed of conflicting elements of experience. The violence and directness of his language reflected the violence of his reactions and the pain of his spirit. His own bitter experience of love probably exacerbated an already sensitive temper to the point where he could no longer maintain the conventional Homeric pose of keeping sexuality in its defined place. He was no mere street corner reductionist, interpreting all life after the fashion of a Priapic poem in order to comfort his own inadequacy by propounding the universal but unacknowledged dominance of the 'lower culture'.[95]

The iambic tradition of crude ridicule may have provided him with the germs of his inspiration to use obscenity in his own secular verses, but his treatment of his subject matter was personal and individual. Obscenity was not a 'safety valve' for his emotions, it was an integrated, operative force in his art of ψόγος. In presenting the contrasts between beauty and foulness, this man of contrasting experiences and ambiguous birthright knows what he is doing, for he is doing what he knows. Modern obscenity has the same purpose as that of Archilochus in making accepted values of behaviour and individual integrity seem unreal and hypocritical in comparison with the facts of sexuality, physical violence, basic bodily functions and behavioural patterns; but Archilochus' scurrilous attacks probably impressed his contemporaries more on account of the Greek view that words had a close connection and continuity with the realities of which they spoke. As far as we know, Archilochus was the first important poet to use 'obscenity' in the particular sense of using words as weapons to dismantle self-respect and reputation. Like some perverse Orpheus, he summoned up in his song a tidal wave from the gutter to engulf his enemies and intimidate his friends. That he sang of other things does not alter either his intention or achievement in this sphere.

VI

POLITICS AND THOUGHT

Both in Paros and Thasos, Archilochus expressed rebellious independence towards his fellows and the world, but he never rejected the importance of his relationship with either, and he seems to have had nothing of the recluse in his personality. Although he was in some ways so fiercely individualist, like other Greeks of his time he was essentially a social creature, and his thoughts about society show little novelty of contents, being distinguished mostly by the violent intensity with which he uttered them. His originality as a 'political thinker' (though such a formulation can hardly be other than an exaggeration in his case), resides in the quality of the feelings which animated his words and his actions, [1] rather than in any inventive new suggestions about the city-state. Much the same may be said of his attitude of life and the human condition in which he and his friends and foes participated.

He was not a systematic thinker; indeed there is no record of any such at this time, but he was a keen observer who possessed great insight. His moral impulses, characteristic of the period in which he lived, reveal themselves as individualist claims that he should be treated justly and honourably. He is convinced that it is just and honourable to retaliate in kind when he has been wronged; or to threaten retaliation as a deterrent in advance of possible humiliations. [2] Love moved him deeply and violently, but it is impossible to say whether the loss of Neoboule or the injury to his honour and self esteem was the more serious hurt to him. His acceptance of the fact of death is typical of the time, and his expression of sympathy to Pericles follows the elegiac theme of endurance and restraint. [3] Age more than death is the enemy of beauty and therefore of life, and his most virulent insults directed against Neoboule and other women ridicule them for being old. [4]

He is said to have lost his fortune in 'political drivelling'.[5] This phrase, quoted by Eusebius, may reflect an hostility to the poet pervading the quotations from Oenomaus' philosophic criticisms of traditional paganism which Eusebius chose to embody to the advantage of Christianity in his own arguments. Its implication of the poet's folly and bad judgement in his political dealings may not simply be latter-day incomprehension of early Greek politics, for the idea of the poet's misfortunes in politics is in harmony with the sketches of his character that we have seen in Pindar and Critias.[6] In spite of his temperamental difficulties in dealing with friends and foes, Archilochus was active in the politics of the time. As Athenaeus makes plain in his remarks which introduce Archilochus' assertion that he serves both Enyalios and the Muses, the poet was proud of the fact that he participated in πολιτικοὶ ἀγῶνες[7]—'contentions concerning the city-state' is the literal meaning of the phrase, and in ancient Greek terms, such conflicts are both internal and external to the state.[8]

Politics in the sense of open, fluid contention between rival groups, involving dialogue, debate and competition both verbal and practical, was a development of the Archaic period,[9] and was characteristic of the age of colonization in which Archilochus lived. We can see the first beginnings of political debate in the second book of the *Iliad*, in which Thersites attempts to oppose his lords in the assembly of the army.[10] The *Iliad*, which was probably put together in its present form in the course of the eighth century B.C., modifies the character of Thersites from its traditional form of a somewhat malignant βασιλεύς from wild Aetolia,[11] to an uproarious man of the people, one of the new men who were beginning to oppose the traditional order at this time. His ferocity and scurrilousness, his ugly person, are all represented in a very unfavourable light. The poet of the epic did not compose for Thersites' social class since it was the aristocracy who were the traditional patrons of poets;[12] but Thersites' rebellious eloquence and his critical attitude are echoed by Archilochus.

In the Thersites episode of the *Iliad* we see the emergence of 'politics' in the later sense of the party competitiveness of the Archaic and classical city-state. In Archilochus we see a more developed stage in the growth of politics, which nonetheless still retain primitive features. As in the *Iliad*, ψόγος remains a recognized element in political debate; indeed we may perhaps infer that ψόγος emerged from ritual into politics in such contexts as that described in the Thersites episode.[13] By Archilochus' time it went beyond the assembly itself, and together with appeals, Hesiodic adjurations, laments and curses (like that, for example, in the 'Strasbourg Epode'),[14] it could make its impact upon the public mind by being circulated at large in song and recitation. Not only is Archilochus capable of sophisticated analysis of a personal situation, like that in the poem 54 T (Pap. Ox. 2310), but we also find him uttering peasant platitudes about relationships between people that are reminiscent of Hesiod's point of view. This primitivism clings to the traditions about his life: witness the story that when he was expelled from the city, a god punished his fellow citizens with sexual impotence. We have already considered his alleged ability to shame people to death by means of his words.

Given his involvement in the life of the πόλις, it is not unreasonable to claim that he is more 'Polisdichter' than condottiere,[15] although it is difficult to discern at all times the role of mercenary from that of enterprising citizen discontented with his own city and hoping for better things in a new colony. Archilochus probably did serve as a mercenary at times, but all of his fragments presupposed involvement in the life of the city-state, whether it be Paros, his home city, or Thasos, where he went to settle, and did not entirely succeed. The πόλις had become the typical ambience of the individual, the amnion within which his personality was sustained.

In this period of movement and new settlements, a change affected but did not overcome the old inherited parameters of Greek life: family, descent, locality and seasonal alternation. The attitude to time was modified—the present, with its actual 'day' of decision and debate, became important.[16] A wanderer, be he mercenary or colonist, never knows in troubled times whether he will see tomorrow. Within the encircling πόλις man competed with man for present gain or glory. Archilochus' fragments show his insight into these features of the society of his time. He sees human personality defined by its ephemeral thought and action rather than by more long-term factors.[17] Man is what he does and thinks. He observes in fg 102 T[18] that the dead really count for very little, and this is a departure from both the heroic veneration of glorious memories,[19] and the chthonic obsessions of Hesiod; but it is to be recalled that the dead in Homer's *Nekyia* are represented as feeble and powerless. In the whirl of competitive life in a πόλις, the dead, no matter how impressive their memorials, soon are proved to be political ineffectives.

More than any parody or specific rejection of the epic ideal or any individualist viewpoint which he expresses in his poetry, it is Archilochus' persistent combativeness which marks him as a new kind of man in the Greek world, the first developed example of his kind known to history. His utterances of anger may in some respects echo the speeches of Achilles and Thersites in their respective expressions of displeasure with authority; but the significant difference is that he is not beaten into silence like Thersites nor does he take himself off to sullen solitude like Achilles.

Archilochus lived in a time when a man could not afford to sulk in his tent, but needed to emerge from it shouting his protests. Persistent and vigorous communication was a staple of political survival, and this kind of politics does not occur in Homer. And yet at the time when Archilochus lived, the prestige of aristocracy was still high, and tradition, irrigated by the ἔπος, was an important component in the image which aristocrats had of themselves, and which society had of them. Archilochus' references to Glaucos illustrate this point.[20]

Archilochus' mixed parentage made it the more likely that in standing between the two worlds of the traditional 'Hesiodic' dispensation and the new 'political' world of contention, colonization and war, he should be conscious both of his own ambiguous identity and of the social gap which he bestrode. It would not be surprising if such a man turned out to be an awkward ally, as well as a ferocious enemy; and his expressions of his personal views were probably so pointed as to generate hostility where he least expected or desired it. As a politician, not as a poet, this trait inevitably involved him in failures, and it is likely that as a politician his judgement was frequently bad, whatever may be said of his principles.

Nowhere is he a more strenuous publicist in his own cause than in the poem fg 54 T (Pap. Ox. 2310):[21]

```
5          ]. . . . .[ ]. .[]. . . . . γὰρ ἐργματ[
           ]. . . . .[ ]. . . . . . . . .ιχα . . ω [
      .].[]ρ.βα. . . . . . . .δε. .[[φ]]ρ ἠμειβόμ[ην·
      "γύνα[ι], φάτιν μὲν τὴν πρὸς ἀνθρώπω[ν κακὴν22
      μὴ τετραμήνηις μηδέν· ἀμφὶ δ'εὐφ[ρόνηι,
10    ἐμοὶ μελήσει· [θ]υμὸν ἵλ[α]ον τίθεο.                    [
      ἐς τοῦτο δή τοι τῆς ἀνολβίης δοκ[έω
      ἥκειν; ἀνήρ τοι δειλὸς ἄρ' ἐφαινόμην[,
      οὐ]δ' οἷός εἰμ' ἐγὼ [ο]ὗτος οὐδ' οἵων ἄπο.      [
      ἐπ]ίσταμαί τοι τὸν φιλ[έο]ν[τα] μὲν φ[ι]λεῖν[,
15    τὸ]ν δ' ἐχθρὸν ἐχθαίρειν τε [κα]ὶ κακο[23
      μύ]ρμηξ. λόγωι νυν τ[ῶιδ' ἀλη]θείη πάρ[α.
      πό]λιν δὲ ταύτη[ν . . .]α[. . . . ἐ]πιστρέ[φεα]ι[
      οὔ]τοι24 ποτ' ἄνδρες ἐξε[πόρθη]σαν, σὺ δ[ὲ
      ν]ῦν εἷλες αἰχμῆι καὶ μέγ' ἐ]ξήρ(ω) κ[λ]έος.
20    κείνης ἄνασσε καὶ τ[υραν]νίην ἔχε·
      π[ο]λ[λοῖ]σ[ὶ θ]η[ν ζ]ηλωτὸς ἀνθρ]ώπων ἔσεαι."
      ]νηΐ σὺν σ[μ]ικρῆι μέγαν
      πόντον περήσ]ας ἦλθες ἐκ Γορτυνίης
      ]. . οτητ . γ . πεστάθη[[ν]]
25    ]καὶ τόδ' ἀρπαλ[ί]ζομ[αι]
      κρ]ηγύης ἀφίκ[
      ]λμοισιν εξ[. . . . . . .] . ς
```

]χεῖρα καὶ π[. .]εστ[ά]θης
]ουσας· φ[ο]ρτίων δὲ μοι μέ[λ]ει
]. ος εἶτ᾽ ἀπώλετο
]ν ἐστι μηχανή

δ᾽ ἂν ἄλ]λον οὗτιν᾽ εὑροίμην ἐγώ
εἰ σ]ὲ κῦμ᾽ ἁλὸς κατέκλυσεν
ἢ   ]. ν χερσὶν αἰχμητέων ὕπο
ἥ]βην ἀγλ[α]ήν ἀπ[ώ]λεσ[α]ς.
νῦν δ᾽   ]θει καί σε θε[ὸς ἐρ]ρύσατο
]·]. κἀμὲ μουνωθέντ᾽ ἰδ . .
]ν, ἐν ζόφωι δὲ κείμενο ⟨ς⟩ [
αὖτις]ἐ[ς] φά[ος κ]ατεστάθην.

These 39 iambic lines probably constitute one poem[25] with a number of different moods and movements rather than a plurality of poems: as far as the broken nature of the remains permit I shall suggest, tentatively, the following version:[26]

5   for works[27]
                         I made answer
       woman do not be in the least apprehensive
       about people's evil gossip. I shall like
10   a woman of good spirits: make your mind cheerful.
       Do I seem to have arrived at such a pitch of misfortune?
       I would seem to be a poor sort of a man indeed,
       and not the kind of man I really am, nor of such decent ancestry.
       I know how to be a friend of him who is my friend and
15   how to hate and satirize(?) an enemy.
       The worm can turn:[28] there's truth in that saying all right.
       this city ----------------- you rule[29]
       never before have men sacked it, but you have
       now taken it with your spear and raised up great fame.
20   Be lord of it and hold unlimited rule over it;[30]
       You will be envied by many of mankind
                            now with a small (ship?)[31]
       having crossed the sea you came from Gortyniē
       (missing abstract word?) + stood?
25   and I grasp this
       --------------------- [32]

       I'm worried about the cargo (?)

(he) is now perished
a means (of escape or recovery?)
never would I find another (such friend?)
if the wave of the sea has washed you down
(or you perished?) by the hands of spearsmen
having destroyed (singular) your happy young life
and a god has saved you
and me left lonely
lying in darkness
has brought again to light

If it is addressed to Neoboule and if Archilochus is speaking to her at a time of crisis in his affairs, he certainly does not exude complete assurance in his own future, but foresees a struggle which he believes he will be able to survive but which involves difficulties for him. He foresees also that a decline in his fortunes, like that which may be alluded to in the fragmentary lines which refer to the loss of a cargo (φορτία), could put an end to his marital plans. The poem is interpretable after this fashion as an unusual specimen of love-letter, half encouraging, half threatening in its attempts to persuade the person addressed not to lose faith in the poet and his future. Not only is the poet's future as an accepted lover at stake, but also, connected with this, his political and financial prospects may be at risk.

The poem is also perhaps not merely 'personal' in a restricted sense of an address to an individual by a poet, but also a piece of propaganda whereby he hopes to refurbish his political 'image' amongst friends and opponents. Love, politics and finance are all aspects of his struggle for distinction, even perhaps for survival, as a citizen in a highly competitive society. All involve either glory or dishonourable and shameful defeat, according to the outcome of his efforts. On these terms he is explaining himself not simply to one woman in the hope that she will understand; he is using his wider, more public, role as poet, which has brought him distinction and which at some point in his career involved him in the ignominy of exile, to convey a message to a general audience, and to show them that he is still a considerable force in his city's public life.

He advises that unfavourable rumours about him should be ignored. The implication would seem to be that he is attempting to mitigate in advance the shame that could arise from his failure and consequential ridicule directed against himself. There is no sign here that he is more concerned with 'internal' valuation of himself by himself rather than prospective 'honour' or 'shame' accorded to him by external opinion. He is not departing from 'shame' society by means of some process of 'conscientious' ethical development. His assertion is the more desperate one that this opinion should be ignored; he does not say that it has no relevance. In this poem it is the ill-disposed opinion of people that is to be ignored.

The other fragment (2 T) in which he rejects public opinion has no context, but neither does it seem to be the harbinger of a new ethos. It too is simply the view of an experienced politician who hopes that eventually the ridicule and shame will die down but dislikes them while they last. It should probably be read with (as an accompanying gloss) his remark that there is a 'ῥυσμός' (105 T), a recurring fluctuation in human affairs.

It is interesting that in Pap. Ox. 2310 he puts his own case as a public personality, a politician, within the formal confines of an expression of personal relationships. In his relationship with Neoboule there may have been a political component—a potentially helpful nexus between himself and the Lycambids if the marriage actually should come about. We cannot be sure about this, but it is a possibility. Then there is a probable allusion in the poem to friendship with a man thought to be lost at sea, but discovered to be safe, whose survival brings great comfort and relief to the poet. The fate of the φορτία[33] which seems to bear upon Archilochus' prospects remains unclear due to the condition of the text, but the final note of optimism would seem to indicate that he had no reason for despair, whether it was recovered or lost.

The tone of this poem is unheroic in its emphasis upon discursive and pragmatic debate. It is heroic in its egotism, however, and in its elements of self-address and self-justification. It is the first example of a naturalistic, arguing poem which we possess in any length, and it seems to echo the character of a political speech, an *apologia* by a politician who finds himself under pressure and strives to explain his position. Most important, it reflects in a realistic way the complexity of life and the varied interplay of motives that affect people in the city state. It does not attack the epic ideal, but it implies its irrelevance; and instead of the fluid temper of the Homeric hero, it presents the image of a more condensed, less compartmentalized personality, who yet has in common with the epic model an impressive and dedicated concern for his own honour.

Conflict was a constant in the life of ancient Greece, and was especially prominent in Archaic Greek experience. The internal turmoil of the πόλεις erupted over the confines of individual states and involved others. Motivations of warfare were in their ostensible forms as many and various as they have been ever since; but economic and territorial jealousies between colonizing πόλεις[34] at this period were frequent material causes for many of the wars, some of which, for instance the so-called Lelantine

War, were very long. Pressures within cities between parties, sometimes representing social groupings, sometimes ethnic layers, sometimes simply traditions, and frequently a mixture of all three, cast out upon the world thousands of adventurers seeking either to join new cities in the making or foreign armies in order to get their living as mercenaries. The foundation of a colony was a means of relieving social congestion of this kind, though it could have a feed-back effect that was uncomfortable for the founding city. And the creation of colonies brought the populations of cities into conflict with one another, as the case seems to have been with the Naxians and the Parians of Thasos (99 T). The roles of wandering mercenary and new colonist probably overlapped in the case of Archilochus, and it was his poetic art that gave this type of a man a voice. His picture of the wandering life is less romantic than that of the *Odyssey*, being not only uncompromising in its naturalism, but brutally bitter.[35]

Archilochus is the first 'war-poet' in the sense of one who treats in his poetry his personal experience as a soldier. His representation of war is that it is mostly squalid and inglorious, involving suffering and loss of life by land and sea. He does not describe a dramatic confrontation of brilliant heroes so much as an unending struggle against hunger and other hardships, alleviated from time to time by a little wine (2 T) and perhaps occasional fornication (143 T), and made endurable in the long term only by a tough soldierly fortitude. The gods lay many burdens on the soldier, as they do upon Hesiod's peasants: their gifts to men, which men are made to administer to their fellows, are death and wounds. Dried out corpses, burning cities covered with a pall of smoke, mutilations,[36] the killing without glory of a few by very many (97 T); all these give the lie to the *Iliadic* image much more than any criticism of the aristocratic life-style of such men as Glaucos. It is by means of the spear, and only the spear, Archilochus says, in a famous elegiac distich, that he gets his living. His bread and his wine depend upon it (2 T), and even when he is resting he has to lean upon it. He is the servant of Enyalios, as well as of the Muses (1 T); war is part of his identity.

Most of his references to war occur in the fragments of his verse which are in tetrameter metre. Here he describes all the destruction, the desiccation of corpses, etc., but if we associate other and not obviously warlike tetrameter fragments with these, we find that in some of them he expresses his longing for Neoboule (111 T); his confusion of mind which can be rectified only by the natural ῥυσμός of the world,[37] and his commiseration with the sad state of a wearied army.[38] It may be that some of these were written when he was on campaign, and that composition of them and their subsequent recital relieved the boredom and hardships which the poet and his comrades endured. This is a possible, but not necessary, inference. The themes are not exclusively warlike, though war predominates in them. The poem beginning χρημάτων ἄελπτον (114 T),[39] which has already been discussed, has no obvious connection with military affairs, at least in the substantial portion of it which survives. Military metaphor, on the other hand, expresses erotic feeling in the fragment 109 T:

> μάχης δὲ τῆς σῆς, ὥστε διψέων πιεῖν,
> ὥς ἐρέω.

> I desire your battle (battle with you) as a thirsty
> man wants drink.

The overlap between war and politics, army and assembly of the people is exemplified in the chant (110 T):

> νῦν δὲ Λεώφιλος μὲν ἄρχει, Λεώφιλος δ' ἐπικρατεῖ
> Λεωφίλῳ δὲ πάντα κεῖται, Λεωφίλου δ' ἀκούεται

> Now Leophilos ('People's Friend') is ruler, Leophilos is in
> power;
> To Leophilos all is entrusted, and Leophilos is listened to.

Probably the name Leophilos was made to suit the activities of a demagogue, a more successful Thersites who has increasing influence with army and colonists. An army could act like a city-state as the assembly of the second book of the *Iliad* indicates; or as was the case much later, in the fifth century B.C., when the Athenian fleet at Samos took on some of the main functions of a πόλις.[41]

While there can be no doubt of his vivid interest in politics and war, it is difficult to define his political policy or to discern his views about how a city should be ruled. Certainly he purports to demand honesty, in public as in private relationships, and we need not doubt his sincerity in this. Whether he leaned more towards democracy or aristocracy it is hard to tell. As we have seen, he himself had some ambitions to rule: power meant success, and honour and happiness which he seems to crave would follow from it. He speaks as an individualist rather than the representative of a party or group, but in political life he needed a group to which he might belong in order to be effective. His maximization of his own sensitive feelings is not unreminiscent of Achilles, or other epic heroes, but unlike these he had no automatic following, no hereditary retainers. Critias' evidence, and that of Eusebius, seem to emphasize his difficult personality and this must have impeded his success as a political leader.

In spite of the apparently radical nature of some of his comments, we have no reason to regard him as convinced that the δῆμος was always right. Yet his criticism of public opinion does not exclude him from the democratic side; nor does the fact of his bastardy or his rejection by the Lycambids necessarily bring him into the radical fold. But his wandering life, and the fact of his engagement in the life of the Thasian colony, would suggest that whatever his personal preferences he was perhaps de facto a democrat, and no doubt involvement in a popular faction would be facilitated rather than hindered by mixed origins. The aristocratic element in him would be likely to increase the respect in which he was held and he could occupy a position that would be much less easy for one who was simply a man of the people—as perhaps we may infer that 'Leophilos' was.

The notion of excessive personal power being held by a Leophilos is obviously repugnant to him, and probably also to many of his fellows. Great elevation of one individual stimulated the competitiveness and spirit of rivalry that were to be found well developed in most Greek males. If we look once more at the iambic poem of fragment 22 T: οὔ μοι τὰ Γύγεω, we observe that the speaker rejects the wealth and power of Gyges, professes himself entirely free from jealousy of these; also he would not presume to feel emulation for the gods, and has no desire for a great τύραννις; such things are very 'far from his eyes'.[42] We then are told, by the Aristotelian context in which the fragment is quoted, that the speaker is a certain Charon, a carpenter.[43] We do not possess the end of the poem itself in which the identity of the narrator as 'Charon' is made clear. Thus we cannot rule out some ironical sentiment such as 'I would not like to be Gyges, but I wouldn't mind having his money'. Yet the lines of the poem that we possess, while they do not suggest that τύραννις was necessarily an evil (Archilochus himself is 'offered' τυραννίη in 54 T), probably assert the virtues of the average decent Hellene in distinction to the luxury of an overweening foreigner, providing a parallel with the ridicule directed at Glaucos for his luxurious way of life. Possibly we may interpret the Gyges poem as propagandist in the sense that it is intended to promote the self-esteem and therefore the political effectiveness of the poet's friends and supporters who would be flattered to think of their own indifference to barbarian flummeries, even those of so rich and powerful a ruler as Gyges. Such a poem, written by a member of an aristocratic house who had need of popular support, would probably be a very acceptable expression of liberal sentiment. It certainly would not harm the position of a 'de facto' democrat. Similarly his poems to Glaucos emphasize the virtues of the plain man, the effective, reliable, but unshowy soldier.[44]

It would be difficult to deduce a general point of view or a philosophy of life from the fragments of Archilochus. Many of his sentiments are current coin of Archaic Greece, and it is his attitude to himself and others in relation to these that is original, rather than any explicitly formulated idea. His group of ἀδύνατα in poem 114 T do not, as has been suggested, represent 'thought'[45] but rather they illustrate an attitude of one of the characters into whose mouth he puts sentiments chosen for the purpose of the poem. No doubt his hatred of war and his unromantic interpretation of its vicissitudes and glories mark him out as distinctive amongst poets, though not, we can be sure, amongst soldiers. He lived in an age in which poets such as Callinus encouraged men to be brave, without such cold-eyed specificity as Archilochus on the subject of war's hardships. Nor was he the first to be hurt by being disappointed of his projected marriage, but he was very probably the first to ventilate his resentment in so fierce and unrelenting a mode. We might fairly say that he saw life as a process of conflict, the incidence of opposite forces and events coming against each other violently and with pain. Friends could not be trusted, for they turned out be betrayers, and faith was easily perjured. Appearances of men and events were deceitful. Private friendships turned sour. War was full of paradox and contradiction, miseries by land and sea, life supported by poor figs as often as by bread and Ismarian wine. Cargoes and loved ones were lost at sea. There was a constant flux of vicissitude which itself could confuse and drown a man's sanity; but the only thing to be done was to face the world bravely, for there was a rhythm in life which involved the compensation of one event by another, and it was necessary therefore to enjoy pleasures and endure ills as they came. This does not imply a belief on his part in some underlying system, some 'pre-Heraclitean' *logos;* it was simply an attitude formed from widely held, somewhat commonplace components. He cannot be considered as an original thinker, though he seems to have possessed a strong and perceptive intelligence. His emphasis upon conflict is not commonplace in that it is firmly based upon his personal experience and observation, and probably reflects an individually distinctive aspect of his personality. His logic is that of the emotions, and the quality of his mind is not to be discerned in such specifically cracker-barrel utterances as 'the fox has many ideas but the hedgehog has one big idea' (196 T). It is deeply encoded in his poetry. The study of the fragments, while it only gives us a partial view, nevertheless suggests that his sense of his own special character was justly founded.

VII

A GENERAL VIEW OF THE FRAGMENTS

It seems appropriate to conclude this discussion of Archilochus with some general comments and a brief over-view of his work as it remains. What is left of his poetry is fragmentary enough, it is sufficient to underwrite the high reputation of his genius in antiquity. From a modern point of view it represents capacity for inventive self-expression, absence of inhibition and technical maturity at an extraordinary stage of development for the seventh century B.C. It is no disrespect to the poet to point out that he had predecessors, and was the successor and beneficiary of a poetic tradition, but his advances upon the *epos* and the Hesiodic poems in terms of emotional freedom and control of poetic material arising from this freedom are remarkable.

Archilochus' mastery of metrical technique in itself shows that he is the inheritor of a process of poetical development.[1] Greek epic metre springs into the sphere of history full developed. We have no clear indications of the preceding stages of its evolution.[2] Probably its development took a long time, but this cannot be said with certainty. Since it can be resolved into semantic and metrical portions or 'formulae', epic hexameter gives some hints about its own earlier stages; but iambic tells us very little about its own possible origin. Archilochus has complete artistic control over epic metre and its 'strophic' offshoot, elegy;[3] and his metrical practice in composing hexameters represents very strict adherence to its rules; he is most particular about the observance of the various metrical 'bridges' whereby word-end is avoided at portions of the verse where its avoidance confirms and strengthens the identity and character of the metre. Similar strictness is observed in his composition of iambics.[4]

The fragments of Callinus,[5] in addition to those of Archilochus in elegy, tend to confirm that metres in the early period varied as to ethos and contents, and that individual rhythms were not clearly associated with particular themes and topics.[6] Although elegy is traditionally associated with the expression of laments and regretful reflections on the unhappier aspects of the human condition, it seems from the start to have been mostly a general purpose metre, and throughout its history as a living genre, it may be said to have retained this character. Archilochus' use of iambic seems to be comparably general, and few subjects would appear to be excluded from his iambic verse. Much the same may be said of his use of the other metrical forms, including those 'strophic' patterns of two or three lines, usually iambic, and of slightly different length, which are characteristic of him and which he devised.

We have mentioned the view that the iambic metre was first used in the worship of Demeter and that it had an inherited association with ψόγος.[7] As the metre closest to the rhythms of ordinary conversation, it became a general medium for Attic tragedy and for the Athenian Old Comedy which was strongly influenced by the tradition of Archilochus. As a metre well suited to dialogue and conversations, it may be said to be well fitted for social or personal satire and ridicule. This emphasis may be observed in Archilochus' iambics. However, his satirical attacks upon people are spread with some impartiality through the other metres in his fragments; and it is the apparent style of rough, swift directness in his iambic trimetra which seems to associate them particularly with ridicule and ψόγος. If we add the 'strophic' blends of lines of his epodes in which elements which we might describe as being of iambic, trochaic and dactylic character are used in various arrangements,[8] then we have a body of material substantially 'iambic' in which emphasis upon personal or critical or abusive subject matter is strong.

It is difficult to decide whether the term 'iambus' is to be strictly attributed to the metrical form, or whether it also applies to the mode or intention of a poem. I think we should not be too strict upon this point: it is hardly insignificant that the *Margites*,[9] which may itself be antecedent to Archilochus, or may be the descendent of a very old genre, should have a blend of dactyl and iambic lines in 'strophic' form. And it also involved a kind of ψόγος.

Very early ancestry for some of the metres of Archilochus is suggested by recent work comparing the metrical forms of various Indo-European languages.[10] Short verses, involving fairly strict syllable counting, can be found in Sanskrit, Slavonic and Old Irish. Seven or eight syllables appear to be typical verse lengths, but they can in some cases be longer—some types go up to eleven. Short strophic alternations, as in some of the combined verse-forms of Archilochus' epodes, are also found in Indo-European verse. It may be that the ancestors of iambic trimeter as well as other shorter verse lengths go back to very early times.[11] These shorter verse-forms in the various languages tend to have a sacral, cultic character; many of them are also gnomic in content (reminding us of that Greek verse-form thought to be the most ancient of all, the paroemiac).[12]

The line of descent cannot be clearly traced, but the comparisons are suggestive. If Archilochus was the 'inventor' of iambic, as some ancient authorities believed him to be,[13] the word must be interpreted not so much in the sense of his being first poet to use the iambic metre, but rather as a poet who gave them a certain individuality of character and direction. He did 'invent', in the more usual sense of that word, certain metres which embodied iambics, and which he used in the 'strophic' stanze of his epodes. It is only in Alexandrian times that we find closer associations between metres and types of subject material,[14] and these associations were in many respects contingent upon the whole classificational enterprise rather than embedded in the early history of the various metres and kinds of poetry.

If we had nothing but Archilochus' elegiac fragments, we would probably find little cause for regarding him as significantly different from Callinus,[15] or Mimnermus. He speaks much the same reflective adaptations of the language of *epos* as these distinguished elegists and his subjects are similar: political comment, expression of his own feelings—the condition of man recognized with quiet grimness.[16] Perhaps his tone of voice is louder and harsher than that of other elegists and his style more sharp and epigrammatic; and maybe it is not entirely chance that has determined that no political exhortation of his, no clarion call to arms survives to compare with Callinus' famous call upon his countrymen to resist Kimmerians.[17] Callinus' fragment admittedly does not convey the poet's conviction that his fellow citizens will pay active attention to his warnings and encouragements; so too there is a dying fall of qualified pessimism in Archilochus' consolation to Pericles.[18] The message of this elegy of Archilochus seems to be that excessive grieving is irrelevant to life: neither feasting nor mourning does anything to change the conditions of life or death, and it is better to set aside grief's excessive manifestations and to suppress the strongest feelings that arise from it. In this example elegy is seen to a limited degree to be the mode, the vehicle of intellectual and moral change. It is protreptic,[19] but the fragments of Archilochus' elegies which deal with politics and war also describe the various experiences themselves in an almost naturalistic fashion.

He makes interesting points about changes in weaponry that have taken place—in the poem about the Eretrians we see this—and we have already discussed the elegiac lines which seek to modify the implications of being a ῥιψάσπις.[20] War is a bringer of grief: the old epic phrase about its 'dread gifts' may possibly assume an ironical overtone in his elegies,[21] but war is a dominant preoccupation of human life as he knows it. Friends in war are friends only so long as they fight. The irrelevance of public opinion (9 T) to a man's own judgement is a soldierly rather than a political sentiment; it may be more than an old elegiac truism in Archilochus' mouth. The fragments of elegy are interpenetrated by the sea which drowns kinsmen,[22] withholds bodies from burial,[23] is grey and terrible, and makes men cringe and pray for safe νόστος.[24] It is a fit metaphor for general experience, as we see elsewhere in Archilochus' poems;[25] but it is not without its pleasures. One of the fragments of elegy mentions drinking on board ship. As we see his poem about the shield, he is very conscious of what he is doing with the verse-form, as he adapts it to argument, makes it the instrument for the expression of new ideas.

Again we may mention parody, when we think of his verses about the soldier's life, and its dependence upon the spear for obtaining bread, good wine, and even something to lean upon while drinking.[26] The phrase ἐν δορί (on or by the spear) is repeated three times in these two lines, the first two occasions indicate a professional 'metaphorical' dependence *on the spear*, the last paronomastically mocks these by referring to actual and physical dependence upon it as something that supports a leaning man. The lines probably are intended to be an allusion to vainglorious soldiers' songs, perhaps we see a representative specimen in the song of Hybrias, the Cretan.[27]

Another fragment, one of his best known, is the elegiac couplet εἰμί δ'ἐγὼ θεράπων, etc., in which he says he is the servitor both of the war-god and of the Muses (1 T).[28] This is a nicely structured pair of lines in which he first mentions himself as the god's θεράπων and follows with a reference to the 'lovely gift' of the Muses, in which he concludes by saying he is an expert. The last word of the couplet ἐπιστάμενος balances the εἰμὶ δ'ἐγώ at the beginning of the first line. The pair of verses begins and ends with references to the poet's own self, bracketing syntactically that self's main enthusiasms. Whether the expression was an independent distich, or two lines originally contained in a larger poem, its tone and contents are reminiscent of an inscription; and it may be a deliberate allusion, possibly parodic, to the style of funerary inscriptions.[29] This is in addition to its more obvious parallel with the egotistic self-introductions of Odysseus and others in the epic.[30] It may also contain a light, ironical allusion to death in the midst of a vigorous assertion of the main activities of his life.

The fragment in which he mentions Pasiphile (16 T) as some kind of whore is the only surviving piece of his elegies which comes close to striking a really angry or obscene note. We have no reason, however, to believe that the specimen was entirely isolated in his elegy, and we bear in mind that his fragment about Pasiphile is not found in an informative context. We do not even know what kind of whoredom he is speaking of; it may even be metaphorical rather than actual—some reference to character which is not strictly sexual. Parallels from elsewhere in his work make such a possibility doubtful, but unhappily we cannot be entirely sure about his intention: the name looks very much like a symbolic concoction (like Leophilos) made up to hide the identity of the object of his comments. This puzzling fragment apart, the fact is that his elegiac remains contain very little ψόγος. Abuse is obviously not excluded, but, if we can infer from the balance of his surviving elegiac lines, he seems to have preferred that it should not be a dominant element in this verse-form.

The themes which occur in his elegies also appear in his iambic. It is fair to say that his iambic poetry treats them in a more direct and immediate fashion, and that we have a clearer impression of the poet speaking in his own voice to us in this less formal metre. Pap. Ox. 2310[31] is a most striking example of this, a frank but complex expression of his own concerns and prospects, which attempts to persuade the addressee of the poem (together with the audience of the poem at large) to take a particular view of the poet's personality. This personal note does not mean that everything that he says about himself is literally authentic in the naive sense of that word. Fantasy is not precluded; but his main interest is that we should interpret his personality according to the image of it which he seeks to project. The question of his sincerity only comes into the matter if we need to decide whether he genuinely wishes us to think of him in the way the poem indicates, or whether he is merely assuming an artistic mask in order to persuade or mislead us into accepting the poem's political implications. There is no ultimate criterion for making such a decision, but reading the poem as it stands suggests to me that he genuinely wants us to see him as a sensitive, ambitious, anxious man, imbued with realism and good sense, but not inhumanly strong; able and energetic, but not without defects; a complicated man who thinks it wise and honest to make himself a plain, direct man in his sentiments—which is very different from merely pretending to be such a person.

The 'Gyges' poem (22 T), for all that it seems to have a sting of paradox in its tail, and to be dramatic representation of the utterance of a certain carpenter called Charon, contributes towards this image of the poet as a frank, undeceived man of ordinary good sense. The nature of the persona chosen for the poem's 'first person' emphasizes this: it is an ordinary man of the people, Charon, who speaks, not Gyges himself or any other great personage. This man-in-the-street has his own distinct views about monarchical magnificence, not flattering ones as the poem shows. This common-sense pose also appears in Archilochus' elegiac assessment of the value of an ἐπίκουρος (15 T): only useful to the extent that he keeps fighting,[32] and it appears in the poems which ridicule Glaucos, and also in the folk wisdom of the Epodes. Pap. Ox. 2310 (54 T) shows that this is an ideal persona, something for which he strives in spite of emotional complexity and self-doubt. In the iambic fragments where we find the poet cursing and satirizing his enemies (and others), he seems to be bringing the pose of plainness to the boundaries of an emotional violence which contradicts it, yet this violence may be said to lend dimension and validity to the 'common-sense' poetry.

The motif of mourning appears in iambic at 19 T where Archilochus speaks of the troubles of the Thasians; also in 20 T, which (like the elegy 10 T) refers to the death of his sister's husband. If we had more contexts for these iambic lines we might see whether the lamentations resembled those of his elegies, or had some differences in style, emphasis or character. Many of his fragments of iambic show him in a far from typically elegiac mode, cursing and satirizing, and, as we have seen, using obscene language to do justice to the violence of his feelings. The fragment (36 T) which possibly describes the self-inflicted death of the Lycambids is in iambic metre; so too the probably obscene 29 T, with its comical playing with sounds (Φρὺξ ἔμυζε). In Pap. Ox. 2310 (54 T) and in the poem concerning Gyges (22 T) there may be seen the beginnings of a kind of poetic conversation, a proto-dramatic style which allows various characters to have their say, not unlike μῖμος, or the αἶνοι which he uses in his epodes.[33] In these and other iambic of Archilochus the predominant note is vigor and ferocity, even though we may discern undertones of insecurity in 54 T. The 'naturalism' of iambic, its closeness to ordinary speech and the lack of formulaic structure are powerfully deployed by him to create sharp and precise effects. Word play, onomatopoeia, and polyptoton balance the apparent immediacy in his expression of strongly felt emotions.[34]

Archilochus' trochaic tetrameters embody a similarly wide range of subject-matter, but if there is a discernible emphasis, it is upon warfare and its vicissitudes. In these fragments he expresses bitterness about war, its experiences and objectives, accompanying this with the 'elegiac' suggestion that it is ultimately the gods who decide all. In the tetrameter there is satire of the over-elegant soldier, Glaucos, criticism of whom we have discussed in relation to Archilochus' views about the epic tradition and the ethos that was derived from it. Archilochus makes strenuous attempts in his tetrameter poetry to come to terms with the squalid and perpetual realities of the wandering soldier's life: the wretchedness of mercenary armies composed of broken, isolated men, the offscourings of Greece,[35] as he calls them; burning towns with smoke rising from them; dried out corpses; the alleged thousand killers of seven dead. War is far from glorious; nor are the dead glorious—they are simply dead. All that can be expected is that the unexpected will happen. Archilochus may have been one of the first poets to see human society as a ship rolling on the waves,[36] but at the same time he left obliged to try to see at least one or two important points about life sharply and steadily.

In 105 T he seems to speak to his own soul, after the fashion of an Homeric hero; he consoles himself in the same fragment with the idea of ῥυσμός, the recurrent rhythm of the world. Confusion is only in the individual's feelings and does not necessarily reflect a universal disorder. Yet he himself has no philosophical pattern to offer; his concern is with individual human experience rather than cosmic design. He knows that it is best to return evil, according to the tradition of inherited Greek ethos. He seems to be convinced that it is better to hold to one reliable idea than to be the fluctuating victim of many. His famous use of the proverbial notion: 'The fox knows many things but the hedgehog knows one important thing' (196 T), indicates that his personal sympathy is with the hedgehog. But as a man of sensitive and subtle mind he knows that it is difficult to attain such simplicity. The unexpected occurs in human relationships, just as in the war (witness the ἀδύνατα of fg 114 T).

In the tetrameters there are also references to love,[37] preponderantly scurrilous, and in this connection the poet mentions his obsession with Neoboule and her family.[38] Although the general emphasis is upon war, wandering, and associated hardships, yet the range of the tetrameter's subject material is almost coextensive with that of the other metrical forms which we have discussed.

The fragments in asynartete metres, the epodes which as a group are formally characterized by brief strophic stanzas of varied metre, are no less varied in their range of topics than those already discussed. Probably the epodes were the best known part of his works in antiquity.[39] They are strongly personal in tone and content, and they show that same element of satire and criticism which Horace imitated in his *Epodes*. Unlike Horace, Archilochus is in a position to name his targets, and as far as may be gathered from the fragmentary state of the material, he seldom fails to hit them squarely. One of his epodes seems to have been a full scale attack upon Lycambes, using the αἶνος of the fox and the eagle[40] to illustrate the treachery which this man is supposed to have used towards him. References in other fragments to this fable, which belongs to the type subsequently called Aesopian,[41] can be brought together to make a tentative adumbration of its argument, which apparently is that no matter how lofty and secure a traitor's retreat may be, he is still accessible to the just vengeance promoted by Zeus.

The αἶνος, in its meaning of animal fable in which the various characteristics of human kind are represented by the salient characteristics of animals, first appears in Greek literature in Hesiod's story of the hawk and the nightingale,[42] a lesson in *Realpolitik* which indicates that a talent for singing is an inadequate defence against a ruthless aggressor. Animal proverbs are to be found in Archilochus elsewhere than in the epodes.[43] If we had more surviving material, it is just possible that evidence for complete αἶνος might emerge in these genres also. The αἶνος is designed to be sharp and surprising in its moral at first impact, but its moral is intended to seem reasonable and acceptable when the hearer has reflected upon it.

Archilochus' iambic poem about Gyges seems to have a characteristic of this kind, though it is not an animal fable, and perhaps we may infer something similar in the poem (114 T), which contains the list of ἀδύνατα, or reversals of the order of nature. In fragment 162 T Archilochus also uses the technique and mannerism of the story-teller:

> Ἐρασμονίδη Χαρίλαε, χρῆμά τοι γελοῖον
> ἐρέω, πολὺ φίλταθ' ἑταίρων, τέρψεαι δ'ἀκούων.

> Charilaos, son of Erasimon, I shall tell you something
> funny, my very good friend, and you will be amused when
>   you hear it.

The poet uses epic phrases,[44] but the style is that of a *logos*;[45] one man is going to tell a story to another, whether it be some anecdote about actual people, or some fable dealing with 'certain' animals;[46] as for instance in the epode (fg. 168 T) 'There is a certain story (αἶνος) amongst people that goes like this: now it happened that a fox and an eagle made a compact. . . .'

In another epode (fg. 188 T), the poet uses the same intimate style: 'I am going to tell you a story, *Kerykides*, bad news; a monkey, sent off by the other animals, went by himself to the edge of the wilderness, and he met a fox who was very cunning.'[47] The story-telling manner is clear enough, but Archilochus did not content himself with simply retailing the λόγος.

He seems to have embodied the fabular elements in the general argument of the poem, and to have interspersed his narratives with apostrophes to his addressee, and with references to the people whom he was identifying with the animal examples.

In Pindar's second *Pythian*, where Archilochus' personality casts a distinct shadow upon the work of the Boeotian poet, we see allusions to the fable of this epode emerging in Pindar's poetic argument. Pindar is at the beginning persuading himself to avoid the satirical savagery of Archilochus, who got no benefit by the practice of it,[48] and then he alludes in the course of the poem to this fable, which has been recalled to his memory by his mention of Archilochus, who made it famous. The point of the fable about the monkey and the fox seems to be that self-knowledge is necessary and that pretensions and exaggerations of one's own importance inevitably lead to disgrace. Pindar's cast of mind as an artist is even more complex, more prone to allusion than that of Archilochus: perhaps he is showing us in the second *Pythian* his own adaptations of the technique used by Archilochus in handling fable material, though of course he does not (he cannot afford to) speak so directly as Archilochus.[49] His mixing of fabular and actual personal references makes effective satire, as well as providing a blended and unified texture for the poem, but like Horace, he does not nominate actual targets.

Although the fragments of Archilochus' epodes are individually small, disjointed and relatively few, we can make out at least this much about their character: they were poems of moralizing and attack, and even on occasion of solemn cursing; as we find in one of the 'Strasbourg' epodes.[50] Archilochus seems to have distilled into his poems of this form his most vehement attacks upon his enemies. Horace, in following him in his own epodes, provides a reflected image of the fierce scurrility which he employed. We cannot relate the fragments of the epodes chronologically to fragments in other metres with any degree of confidence, but it might be reasonable to suggest that they represent his work in a mature and complex state of development. Not only do Horace's imitations give us their adumbrated impression of the originals: in the poem of the Cologne Papyrus we at least see this kind of Archilochian poetry as it was in fact (if the poem be held to be genuine), or at least as it was seen by a clever imitator of the original.[51] The Cologne Papyrus does not contain αἶνος, it simply tells its vicious story with a multiplicity of cutting edges to lacerate its victims.

It is by means of 'conversation' or dialogue in this poem, rather than startling imagery, that Archilochus obtains his effects. Plain circumstantial description comes out of the conversation and this effectively sets the scene in this poem. The 'characters' talk themselves towards the psy-

chological (and sexual) climax at the end of the poem, and its effect of
emotional stress in its movement is wound up by the use of suggestive
'kennings' that represent sexual ideas.[52] The metre is 'strophic',[53] but the
character of the poetry, as in the case of other epodic fragments, has much
in common with logos, and it foreshadows in vocabulary and manner the
iambic and trochaic verse of the poets of Old Comedy.

Archilochus could coin a powerful image when artistic need de-
manded, as in his likening of the mountain ridge on an island to the 'back-
bone of an ass' (ὄνου ῥάχις, 17 T); and his fragments contain examples of
that cross-infection from one metaphorical image to another that M. S.
Silk has recently discussed under the name of poetic 'interaction.'[54] But in
general it is by the sheer energy of his feeling that Archilochus stakes his
artistic claim, an energy which suffuses both the plain and epic-inspired
elements of his diction and welds them into something new, and fresh,
and entirely individual. His secret is that he aims at expressing rather
than elaborating his feelings. He conveys immediacy, whether it be the
animality of some sexually explicit scene, or the smoke rising from a de-
stroyed town.

Any attempt at literary evaluation of a set of poetic fragments involves
what we might call the 'lapidary problem'. I mean by this the risk of mis-
understanding that comes from the impression of epigrammatic neatness
that the mere fact of being fragmentary can sometimes confer upon poetic
fragments. Statements, ideas, and images in the absence of their lost con-
texts can appear to stand out boldly in a semantic relief, and they can
seem thereby to be much more significant than they might possibly be if
we possessed the lines and words which originally surrounded them. Re-
lated to this problem is that which concerns especially the Papyrus frag-
ments and which comes from the interstices that occur in longer frag-
ments. These, like the holes in a sculpture of Henry Moore, challenge our
capacity for inference. It is too easy to forget that the apertures in a piece
of modern sculpture are by design, while the gaps in a literary fragment
are accidental. The reference to sculpture is not completely metaphorical,
for the visual impact of fragments, particularly in a printed book, is cap-
able of achieving its own deceptive impression.[55] Ezra Pound made a
deliberate and ingenious use of this *trompe l'oeil* when he made the fol-
lowing poem out of a few words on papyrus:

> Spring
> too long
> Gongyla.[56]

But we must not let caution strangle all inference at birth, for attempts at the reconstruction of the meanings of the two long poems which have been discussed in preceding chapters are necessary to the gradual progress of literary criticism of ancient literature, even though they necessarily contain an element of inference which probably will be superseded. Speculative interpretation in the absence of a sufficiency of facts is a simple necessity for those who study poets whose work remains only in fragments, but if it is not attempted, the study of such material must remain almost entirely grammatical and linguistic. It is difficult at times to prevent literary interpretation of these fragments from becoming itself a kind of creative writing, but even where this happens, it is healthier and more advantageous to the interests of ancient poetry to prune speculation that has grown too boldly than to repress it.

In spite of Archilochus' fame in antiquity, and the influence which he exercised on other poets of the ancient world, he has had very little impact upon the modern literary world outside the field of classical scholarship. Within Classics, he has been for the most part a name to which certain interesting and racy associations were attached—at least until longer papyrus fragments began to underwrite his reputation more firmly and to show us more of what he could do. The public at large remained largely ignorant of him, although its awareness of Homer and Euripides was considerable. We can point to the difficulty of translating scattered fragments convincingly as one principal cause of his remaining so obscure. And there was none of the aura of romance surrounding his name which has recommended Sappho to modern attention. Archilochus was by the nature of his personality an 'outsider' and his individualism isolated him not only in his own times, but in ours. Had he been more sympathetic as a poetic persona, his work would probably have survived in greater bulk from later antiquity. As it is, we cannot produce translations of him of the kind that have made Homer a best-seller in English in this century.

So it is not surprising that when Guy Davenport produced his translation of Archilochus,[57] there were some who thought that the ancient poet's personality was merely an invention of the modern poet, and that the idea of this material being a 'translation' was part of an ingenious poetic attitude devised by Davenport to achieve a particular modality of expression.[58] This impression was increased by the gulf which separated these vigorously American epigrams (for the fragments were translated most effectively into the American idiom), from the 'Swinburnian Greece' of the modern English-speaking imagination. Not only are we reminded of Ezra Pound's homiletic tone; there is also an extended use of Pound's clever idea of using space (or emptiness) for poetic effect.

The treatment of the fragments in Davenport's translation is 'synchronic' rather than 'diachronic': he makes no concessions at all to the millennia which separate both himself and modern America from the Archaic Greek poet, or the peculiar history which moulded Archilochus' personality. His words are instinct with the history of our own century and they necessarily impose some of the assumptions of our contemporary language upon the words of the seventh century B.C. This disregard of perspective raises a number of topics, some of them semantic, some of them literary, and some also educational, which it is not proposed to discuss at present. However, Davenport's approach does bring a most important element of immediacy and life into modern notions of early Greek poetry, and he brings to realization his obviously deeply-felt desire to interpret poetry by poetry, and as poetry. Thus the translation becomes an act of literary creation in its own right, rather than a mere 'version'.

I do not know whether this would work in the case of all ancient poets: I can imagine that Aratus or Nicander or the like might provide difficulties which such a technique could hardly overcome. Yet with Archilochus, it is undoubtedly a success, and this is not merely a matter of the translator's talent; it arises from the nature of Archilochus and his work. You can do this kind of translation, which amounts almost to a three-dimensional practical criticism of the poems, when the poet is speaking as a person, especially a person who convincingly represents individual and sincere directness. History can be set aside in such circumstances because there is a continuum of feeling between Archilochus and ourselves which the poet's own intensity generates. We have learned in our own century what chaos, revolution, war and general disturbance of society mean, and his words raise echoes when they are translated into our idiom. This is not to say that we can understand him fully as a poet or a phenomenon of literary history without persistent and imaginative enquiry into the remaining historical facts about him and his times. It simply means that his far-off voice speaks of a scheme of things which is not entirely alien to us, though the line of connection has been buried deep in the intervening centuries.

Modern brutality of utterance is well-suited to rendering his ideas for the present age. He combined the life of action with the intellectual life, running to extremes in both aspects of his experience. He is a unitary man, and he comprehends and expresses the connection between the promptings of his genitals and the operations of politics and war. He makes little or no difference in the level of intensity and interest that he applies to explaining himself in every sphere of his life. He is the opposite of the impersonality of *epos*, and he makes it his concern to adapt *epos* to the life and experience of his time, giving it an immediacy which already in the seventh century B.C. seemed to be alien to its lofty heroism. His interpretation of *epos* subjected it to the most severe tests that its reputation has ever endured, since it was by the standards of life, not myth, that he measured it.

There is hardly an articulated fragment of his work which does not suggest a vivid idea impinging upon his mind, and it would scarcely be unreasonable for us to regard him as one of those rare artists who continued to be susceptible to new and fresh impressions throughout their lives. His response to the impressions of his senses seems particularly strong,[59] but his central core of consciousness never seems to be overwhelmed, and his voice, even in expressing despair, has the confidence of intelligent, creative man. He was a master of poetic technique, but his greatest asset as a poet is, I believe, a personality which enabled him to give a clear and powerful expression to some of the most basic human emotions and experiences. It is this characteristic in him which confers a strange modernity upon him, and enables him to speak to us more directly even than Sappho or Alcaeus. He did not seek to impose an artificial pattern upon the period of social flux in which he lived, but spoke of things as he saw them, with a frankness and clarity of vision that is to be seen later in his fellow Ionians, the φυσιολογοί of Miletus, who attempted to explain the universe which they saw with their own eyes, and not that which was increased with the ornaments of inherited μῦθος. Seldom has a frontier society had a man of such genius to represent its life to itself and to posterity.

LIST OF ABBREVIATIONS

AAWW	*Anzeiger der Akademie der Wissenschaften in Wien*
A Ant Hung	*Acta Antiqua Academiae Scientiarum Hungaricae*
AJP	*American Journal of Philology*
Anacreon	**Anacreon, Fragmenta**, edidit etc. **Bruno Gentili;** **Lyricorum Graecorum quae exstant**, vol. 1 (Rome 1958)
AP	*Anthologia Palatina*
Arkh Eph	*Arkhaiologike Ephemeris*
B	*Poetae Lyrici Graeci*, ed. Th. Bergk, vol. 2 (Leipzig 1915) 4th edition
Barns	J. Barns, 'A New Gnomologium, with some remarks on Gnomic Anthologies', *CQ* 44 (1950) 126-137; part 2,45 (1951) 1-19
BIEH	*Boletín del Instituto de Estudios Helénicos*
Blass	F. Blass, *Die Attische Beredsamkeit*
Blumenthal	A. von Blumenthal, *Die Schätzung des Archilochos im Altertume* (Stuttgart 1922)
Bond	G. W. Bond, 'Archilochus and the Lycambides, A New Literary Fragment', *Hermathena* 80 (1952) 1-11
Breitenstein	**T. Breitenstein, 'Hésiode et Archiloque',** *Odense University Classical Studies* 1 (1971)
Broccia	G. Broccia, ΠΟΘΟΣ e ΨΟΓΟΣ, *il frammento 6D e l'opera di Archiloco* (Rome 1959)
Cherniss	H. F. Cherniss, 'Me ex versiculis meis parum pudicum', *Critical Essays on Roman Literature*, edited by J. P. Sullivan (London 1962), pp. 15-30
CJ	*Classical Journal*
Col Pap	*Papyrus Coloniensis* inv. 7511 (the fragment published by Merkelbach and West in *ZPE* 14 [1974])
Cope	E. M. Cope, *The Rhetoric of Aristotle* (Cambridge 1877)

Costanza	S. Costanza, 'Interpretazione di Fr 25 D di Archiloco', *Università di Messina Facoltà di Lettere e Filosofia* (1950), pp. 152-61.
CP	*Classical Philology*
CQ	*Classical Quarterly*
CR	*Classical Review*
D	E. Diehl, *Anthologia Lyrica* (Leipzig 1922)
Davenport	G. Davenport, *Archilochus*, translated, with a foreword by Hugh Kenner (Calif. 1963)
Davison	J. A. Davison, 'Quotations and Allusions in Early Greek Literature', *Eranos* 53 (1955) 124-39
Diels-Kranz	H. Diels, *Die Fragmente der Vorsokratiker, Griechisch und Deutsch, herausgegeben von Walther Kranz* (Berlin 1972)
Donlan	Walter Donlan, 'Archilochus, Strabo and the Lelantine War', *TAPA* 101 (1970) 131-42
Edmonds	J. M. Edmonds, *The Fragments of Greek Comedy*, vols. 1-3a (Leiden 1957–61)
Elliott, *Power*	R. C. Elliott, *The Power of Satire* (Princeton 1960)
Elliott, *Satire*	R. C. Elliott, 'Satire und Magie', *Antaios* 4 (1962) 313-26
Entretiens	*Entretiens sur l'Antiquité Classique: Fondation Hardt*, Tome 10 (1964), 'Archiloque'
Forrest	W. G. Forrest, *The Emergence of Greek Democracy* (London 1966)
Fotheringham	J. K. Fotheringham, *Memoirs of the National Royal Astronomical Society* 81, 2 (1920) 104-26
Fraenkel, *Aeschylus*	E. Fraenkel, *Aeschylus, Agamemnon*, edited with a commentary (Oxford 1950)
Fraenkel, *JRS*	E. Fraenkel, 'Two Poems of Catullus', *Journal of Roman Studies* 51 (1961) 46-53
Fränkel, *Dichtung*	H. Fränkel, *Dichtung und Philosophie des Frühen Griechentums* (New York 1951)
Frazer	J. G. Frazer, *The Golden Bough, A Study in Magic and Religion*
Gallavotti	C. Gallavotti, 'Archiloco', *PP* (1949) 130-53
Geiger	G. Geiger, *De Callini Elegiarum Scriptoris Aetate* (Erlangen 1877)
Gentili	Bruno Gentili, 'Interpretazione di Archiloco fr 2D = 7LB', *RFIC* 93 (1965) 129-34

Gerevini   S. Gerevini, "L'Archiloco perduto e la tradizione
                    critica literaria', *Parola del Passato* 9 (1954)
                    256-64

Gerlach   W. Gerlach, 'Staat und Staatschiff', *Gymnasium*
                    (1937) 128ff

Gouldner   A. W. Gouldner, *Enter Plato* (London 1965)

Grant   **Mary A. Grant, Folk-Tale and Hero-Tale Motifs in
                    the Odes of Pindar (Kansas 1967)**

Grassmann   V. Grassmann, *Die Erotischen Epoden des Horaz,
                    Literarischer Hintergrund und Sprachliche Tradi-
                    tion* (Munich 1966)

GRBS   *Greek, Roman and Byzantine Studies*

Grube   G. M. A. Grube, *The Greek and Roman Critics*
                    (London 1965)

Guthrie   W. K. C. Guthrie, *A History of Greek Philosophy*
                    (Cambridge 1962–69)

Hauvette   A. Hauvette, *Archiloque, sa vie et ses poésies* (Paris
                    1905)

Hendrickson   G. L. Hendrickson 'Archilochus and the victims
                    of his Iambics', *AJP* 46 (1925) 101-27

*Honour and   *Honour and Shame, The Values of Mediterranean
    Shame*   Society*, edited by J. G. Peristiany (Nature of
                    Human Society Series, London 1965)

HSCP   *Harvard Studies in Classical Philology*

IG   *Inscriptiones Graecae*, 1873-

Jacoby,   F. Jacoby, *Apollodors Chronik Eine Sammlung der
    Apollodors   Fragmente* (Berlin 1902)

Jacoby, *CQ*   F. Jacoby, *CQ* 35 (1941) 97-109

Jacoby, *FGH*   F. Jacoby, *Die Fragmente der Griechischen Histor-
                    iker*, part 3

Jeffrey   L. H. Jeffrey, *The Local Scripts of Archaic Greece*
                    (Oxford 1961)

Kirchner   J. Kirchner, *Prosopographia Attica*

Kirk   G. S. Kirk, *Heraclitus, The Cosmic Fragments*
                    Cambridge 1954)

Kontoleon,   N. Kontoleon, 'Neai Epigraphai peri tou Ar-
    Arkh Eph   khilokhou ek Parou', *Arkh Eph* 91 (1952) 32-95

Kontoleon   N. Kontoleon, 'Archilochos und Paros', *Entre-
    Entretiens   tiens*, pp. 39-86

Krumbacher   K. Krumbacher, *Geschichte der Byzantinischen
                    Literatur 527–1453* B.C. (*Müller Handbuch*, ed. 2)

Lacey	W. K. Lacey, *The Family in Classical Greece* (London 1968)
Langerbeck	H. Landerbeck, 'Margites', *HSCP* 72 (1958) 33-62
Lasserre	F. Lasserre, *Les Épodes d'Archiloque* (Paris 1950)
L/B	F. Lasserre and A. Bonnard, *Archiloque Fragments* (Paris 1958)
Lesky	Albin Lesky, *A History of Greek Literature*, translated by C. de Heer and J. A. Willis (London 1966)
Liebel	*Archilochi Iambographorum Principis Reliquiae quas accuratius collegit Adnotationibus Variorum Doctorum suisque Animadversionibus illustravit ex praemissa De Vita et Scriptis Poetae Commentatione nunc seorsum*, edidit Ignatius Liebel (Leipzig 1812)
Maas	P. Maas, *Greek Metre*, translated by H. Lloyd-Jones (Oxford 1962)
Marcovich	M. Marcovich, 'A New Poem of Archilochus P. Colon Inv. 7511', *GRBS* 16, 1 (1975) 5-14
Marcuse	Ludwig Marcuse, *Obscene, the History of an Indignation*, translated by Karen Gershen, (London 1965)
Marzullo	B. Marzullo, 'La Chioma di Neoboule', *RhM* (1957) 68-82
Masson	O. Masson, 'Les Épodes de Strasbourg', *REG* 59 (1946–47) 8-27; 'Encore Les Épodes de Strasbourg', *REG* 64 (1951) 427-442
Merkelbach and West	R. Merkelbach and M. L. West, 'Ein Archilochus-Papyrus', *Zeitschrift für Papyrologie und Epigraphik* 14 (1974) 97-113
Mnes. Inscr.	*Mnesiepis Inscriptio*, Tarditi, *Archilochus*, p. 4 ff
Mus. Cr.	*Museum Criticum Quaderni Dell'Istituto Di Filologia Classica Dell'Università di Bologna* 8-9 (1973–74)
Nestle	W. Nestle, 'Kritias, Eine Studie', *Neue Jahrbücher für das Klassische Altertum* (1903) 81-107 and 178-99
Notopoulos	J. A. Notopoulos, 'Homer, Hesiod and the Achaean Heritage of Oral Poetry', *Hesperia* 29 (1960) 177-97
Ninck	Martin Ninck, *Die Bedeutung des Wassers im Kult und Leben der Alten* (Leipzig 1921, reprinted Darmstadt 1968)

Oppolzer	Th. von Oppolzer, 'Canon der Finsternisse', *Mathematisch-Naturwissenschaftliche Classe der Kaiserlichen Akademie der Wissenschaften* (Vienna 1887)
Pape-Benseler	W. Pape and C. Benseler, *Wörterbuch der Griechischen Eigennamen* (reprint Graz 1959)
Pap. Herc.	*Herculanensium voluminum quae supersunt*, C.A. 1-11 (Naples 1862–76)
Pap. Ox.	*The Papyri from Oxyrhynchus*, published by the Egypt Exploration Society, (London 1898-)
Parke	H. W. Parke, 'The Newly Discovered Delphic Responses from Paros', *CQ* 8 (1958) 90-94
Parke and Wormell	H. W. Parke and D. E. W. Wormell, *The Delphic Oracle* (Oxford 1956)
Parry	Milman Parry, *The Making of Homeric Verse, The Collected Papers of Milman Parry*, edited by Adam Parry (Oxford 1971), p. 13
Pasquali	G. Pasquali, 'Leggendo II', *SIFC* 6 (1929)
PCPhS	*Proceedings of the Cambridge Philological Society*
Pfeiffer	R. Pfeiffer, *A History of Classical Scholarship* (Oxford 1968)
Piccolomini	A. Piccolomini, 'Quaestionum de Archilocho capita tria', *Hermes* 18 (1883) 264 ff
PMLA	*Proceedings of the Modern Languages Association of America*
PP	*La Parola del Passato, Rivista di Studi Classici*
QUCC	*Quaderni Urbinati di Cultura Classica*
Rankin, *Emerita* (1972)	H. D. Rankin, 'Archilochus Fg. 2 D: Fg. 7 (L-B)', *Emerita* 40 (1972) 469-79
Rankin, *Emerita* (1975)	H. D. Rankin, 'Archilochus in Pindar *Pythian* 2', *Emerita* 43 (1975) 249-55
Rankin, *Eos*	H. D. Rankin, 'Archilochus was no magician', *Eos* 19 (1974) 5-21
Rankin, *Eranos*	H. D. Rankin, 'Archilochus (*Pap. Ox.* 2310 Fr 1 Col 1)', *Eranos* 72 (1974) 1-15
Rankin, *GB*	H. D. Rankin, 'ΜΟΙΧΟΣ, ΛΑΓΝΟΣ ΚΑΙ ΥΒΡΙΣΤΗΕ, Critias and his criticism of Archilochus', *Grazer Beiträge* 3 (1975) 323-34
Rankin, *Hermathena*	H. D. Rankin, 'Archilochus and Achilles', *Hermathena H. W. Parke Festschrift* 118 (1974) 91-98
Rankin, *Symbolae*	H. D. Rankin, 'Thersites the Malcontent', *Symbolae Osloenses* 48 (1972) 36-60

RCCM	*Rivista di Cultura Classica e Medioevale*
RE	Pauly-Wissowa, *Real-Encyclopädie der Classischen Altertumswissenschaft*
REG	*Revue des Études Grecques*
RFIC	*Rivista di filologia e istruzione classica*
RhM	*Rheinisches Museum für Philologie*
RIL	*Rendiconti dell'Istituto Lombardo Classe di Lettere Scienze morali e storiche*
RSA	*Rivista di Storia Antica e di Scienze Affini*
Russell	D. A. Russell, *Longinus on the Sublime* (Oxford 1969)
Schlonsky	T. Schlonsky, 'Literary Parody, Remarks on its Method and Function', *Proceedings of the Fourth Congress of the International Comparative Literature Association*
Schmid-Stählin	W. Schmid and Otto Stählin, *Geschichte der Griechischen Literatur* (Munich 1929)
Semerano	G. Semerano, 'Archiloco nel giudizio del passato', *Maia* (1951) 167-86
SIFC	*Studi Italiani di Filologia Classica*
TAPA	*Transactions of the American Philological Association*
Taillardat	J. Taillardat, *Les Images d'Aristophane Étude de Langue et de Style* (Paris 1965)
Tarditi, *Archil.*	G. Tarditi, *Archilochus, Fragmenta edidit, Veterum testimonia collegit Iohannes Tarditi, Lyricorum Graecorum quae extant*, vol. 2 (Rome 1968)
Tarditi, *PP*	G. Tarditi, 'La nuova epigrafe archilochea e la tradizione biografica del poeta', *PP* 47 (1956) 122-39
Tarditi, *RFIC*	G. Tarditi, 'In margine alla cronologia di Archiloco', *RFIC* 37 (1959) 113-18
Terzaghi	N. Terzaghi, 'Abiecta non bene parmula', *Bollettino di Filologia Classica* 3 (1928) 23-24
Thompson	J. A. K. Thompson, *The Art of the Logos* (London 1935)
Travis	J. Travis, 'A Druidic Prophecy, the First Irish Satire and a Poem to Raise Blisters', *PMLA* 57 4, 1 (December 1942), 901-15
Treu	Archilochos, Griechisch und Deutsch herausgegeben von Max Treu (Munich 1959)

Toy — *Studies in the History of Religions presented to Crawford Howell Toy* (New York 1912)

Vendryes — J. Vendryes, Review of F. N. Robinson's '*Satirists and Enchanters in Early Irish Literature*', *Revue Celtique* 34 (1913) 94-96

Walcot — P. Walcot, *Greek Peasants Ancient and Modern* (Manchester 1970)

Watkins — C. Watkins, 'Indo-European Metres and Archaic Irish Verse', *Celtica* 6 (1963) 194-249

West, *CQ* — M. L. West, 'Greek Poetry 2000 B.C.–700 B.C.', *CQ* 23 (1974) 179-92

West, *Glotta* — M. L. West, 'Indo-European Metre', *Glotta* 51 (1973) 161-87

Whitman — C. H. Whitman, *Aristophanes and the Comic Hero* (Cambridge, Mass. 1964)

Wolf — F. Wolf, *Untersuchungen zu Archilochos' Epoden*, Dissertation, Halle-Wittenburg 1966

WUS — *Washington University Studies*

Zeller — E. Zeller, *Die Philosophie der Griechen in Ihrer Geschichtlichen Entwicklung*

ZPE — *Zeitschrift für Papyrologie und Epigraphik*

Appendix

Col. Pap. 7511

1. Merkelbach and West, Marcovich, Barigazzi *Mus. Cr.*, Gallavotti *Mus. Cr.*, J. Ebert, and W. Luppe in *ZPE* 16 (1975) 222-233, seem to accept that the poem is (1) archaic (2) probably of Archilochus. Marzullo *Mus. Cr.* and T. Gelzer (in a paper to the Joint Meeting of Hellenic and Roman Societies, August 8th, Oxford 1975) are sceptical, regarding it as an imitative concoction made up in later centuries.

2. Imitations of Archilochus (or let us rather say, imitations and essays in his style) are not unexampled in Hellenistic and later times: G. Coppola, *SIFC* 7 (1929) 155-68; G. Pasquali, *SIFC* 10 (1933) 169-75; Coppola, *SIFC* 10 (1933) 165-68; Bond, *Hermath* 130 (1952) 1-11; H. Lloyd-Jones, *PCPhS* 182 (1952–53) 36-43; G. Tarditi, *RCCM* 3 (1961) 311-16; C. Calame *QUCC* 1, 2 (1966) 120.

3. Arguments against Archilochean authorship based upon the view that the vocabulary of the poem is not such as A would have had available or would have used (Marzullo, Gelzer) are persuasive, but their validity is limited by the small sample of Archaic Greek literature that has survived. Apart from the Homeric (and Hesiodic) poems to which the fragments of Archilochus stand in a somewhat individual relationship, there is very little literature remaining from the Archaic period, certainly not enough to enable us to make a conclusive judgement upon the poem's authenticity on these grounds.

4. The poem's language and treatment of theme are reminiscent of the *Dios Apatē* episode of the *Iliad* 14, 292-251 (F. Bossi *Mus. Cr.*). The Homeric influence is to be expected in A, and thus does not constitute an argument against the poem's authenticity, especially since the verbal influence of the *epos* seems to be well assimilated rather than crudely obvious. It is reasonable that A should, perhaps ironically, allude to this Olympian love-game as a *metron* for his own squalidly human affair. Further the *Dios Apatē* and the *Col Pap* poem have common ground in heartlessness and ulterior motive on the part of the principals in their respective scenes. It is doubtful whether an imitator would use an Homeric idea so ingeniously.

5. While it is clear that the poem has a certain unevenness and an element of staccato in its construction, this need not be against its authenticity. In tone and attitude it is reminiscent of the half-confident, half-nervous 'first person' of *Pap. Ox.* 2310, which most people regard as genuinely of A. Also the *Col Pap* poem has the blend of brutality and aesthesis which

seems characteristic of A—admittedly this would be capable of being imitated, but I think the staccato I mentioned is too bold and deliberate to suggest an imitator.

6. In spite of 2, above, I think that the burden of proof that the poem is an imitation lies upon those who argue this, and I do not believe that burden to be discharged by the arguments relating to vocabulary, etc. We do not know for certain whether the epodic fragment 80 D (*Pap. Argent*) which is not generally accepted[1] as genuinely of Archilochus, was actually and deliberately composed in imitation of him, by whom or when. The background and motivation of an imitator, and his intention as a composer, poses as valid a literary question as in the case of any other author. In spite of some lack of concinnity, the poem seems to be of too high a quality for the suggestion that it is an imitation to be *prima facie* convincing.

7. But if as sceptics we proposed a minimal hyphthesis: that the poem is an imitation or version by somebody who knew the poetry and tradition of Archilochus very well (the poem squares with Critias' account of the poet: Gallavotti *Mus. Cr.* 22); then we may infer from it some useful points about the actual poetry of Archilochus upon which it was based.

8. The whole question remains inconclusive, and it may never be finally settled. I personally accept the view that the poem is of Archilochus, but I appreciate the doubts expressed by others. The minimum hypothesis (7 above) is useful to us, but for literary assessment of the 'original' work of Archilochus it could hardly serve. In the present state of knowledge it is subjective literary judgement of the individual that determines (for him) whether he accepts the poem as one of Archilochus'.

NOTES

1. The question of the Strasbourg Epodes is not yet completely settled. Diehl prints all of them; Tarditi accepts one, and L/B omit them. For a recent resume of the question which takes a moderately positive line, G. M. Kirkwood *TAPA* 92 (1961) 267-282. For various aspects of the discussion R. Reitzenstein, 'Zwei Neue Fragmente der Epoden des Archilochos', *Berliner Sitzungsber.* (1889) 857-64; G. Pasquali, *SIFC* 7 (1929) 307-377; V. Galli, *Atene e Roma* 6 (1938) 157-75; 8 (1940) 255-67; G. Perotta *SIFC* 16 (1939) 177; 88; R. Cantarella, *Aegyptus* (1944) 19; O. Masson *REG* (1946–47) 8-17; C. Del Grande, *REG* (1951) 427-42, *Giornale Ital. di Filologia* 1 (1948) 255-57; V. Klinger *Eos* 63 (1948) 40-47; G. Morelli *Maia* 2 (1952) 256-57. Problems of vocabulary arise which are reminiscent of difficulties adduced about the Cologne poem; also the question of metre. Again it is difficult to be conclusive. The first Strasbourg Epode is very probably genuinely of A's authorship, but the remaining fragment is doubtful, possibly of Hipponax, though this would seem to be opposed by a possible reference to it in Alcaeus (Kirkwood 280); on the question of poems by different authors presented in anthologies, J. Barns, *CQ* 44 (1950), 126-137 and *CQ* 45 (1951), 1-19.

NOTES

CHAPTER 1

The edition principally used in these notes will be that of G. Tarditi, *Archilochus, Fragmenta edidit Veterum testimonia collegit Iohannes Tarditi, Lyricorum Graecorum quae extant*, Vol. II (Rome 1968), and references to fragments contained in it will consist of a number followed by T. Other references will be found to relate to other editions, e.g. *Archiloque, Fragments*, ed. by F. Lasserre and A. Bonnard (Paris 1958), indicated by a number followed by L/B; E. Diehl, *Anthologia Lyrica* (Leipzig 1922), number of the fragment followed by D; Th. Bergk, *Poetae Lyrici Graeci* (Leipzig 1915), ed.4) number of the fragment followed by B.

1. Semerano, p. 169.
2. Whitman, p. 38.
3. Plutarch *Inst. Lac.* 239 b; Valerius Maximus 6,3.
4. *Index Hesychii operum Aristotelis* 144: there were three books, presumably one devoted to each of the authors.
5. 'The Writer on the Sublime' (Longinus) 13.3: Archilochus is in the class of poets who are 'most Homeric'; cf. Velleius Paterculus 1.5. There are many references in which Archilochus is mentioned together with Homer. For a list of these see Tarditi, p. 233. For Hesiod, Plato *Ion* 531a-532a; Plutarch *Numa* 62c; also V. Steffen's discussion, 'De Archilocho Quasi Naturali Hesiodi Aemulatore', *Eos* 46 (1952–53) 33-48; also G. Setti, 'Omero ed Archiloco', *RSA* 2, fasc. 4.
6. Velleius Paterculus 1,5. He is regarded as the inventor of iambic by Clement of Alexandria *Strom* 1.16.79; Ovid *Ibis* 521; schol on Lucian *Bis Accusatus*, p. 146. It may be debated whether they literally mean that he first used this metrical form or first gave it a definitive and polished use. See K. J. Dover, 'The Poetry of Archilochus', *Entretiens* 10 (1964) 183-222.
7. Grube, pp. 8-9, 27-28, and passim.
8. Alcidamas, quoted at Aristotle *Rhetoric* 1398 b ii; he was a pupil of Gorgias. See further Guthrie, vol. 3, *The Fifth-Century Enlightenment*, pp. 311-13.
9. Kontoleon, *Arkh. Eph.* and *Entretiens*; also E. Vanderpool, *AJP* 76 (1955) 186-88; G. Tarditi, *PP*; H. W. Parke, *CQ* 8 (1958) 90-94.
10. *The Monumentum Archilocheion* published by Hiller von Gaertringen: *IG* XII 5,1 (1903); XII 5,2 (1909). Jacoby, *FGH*, pp. B 479-80 on Demeas, also B 420-422; for the list of fundamental works of Hiller von Gaertringen on this inscription, Treu, p. 143. The scene depicted on the 'Boston Pyxis' may indicate that Archilochus' life story was known in Athens as early as 460 B.C.: Kontoleon, *Arkh. Eph.*, p. 48; *Entretiens*, p. 47.
11. Diogenes Laertius ix.i: Diels-Kranz, Heraclitus, fg 42: Guthrie, vol. 1, *The Earlier Presocratics and the Pythagoreans*, pp. 412-13, see H's criticism as being directed towards Archil. fg 68 D (107T), which says 'Men's minds, Glaucus, son of Leptines, are just as Zeus may ordain day by day', a sentiment which follows *Od* 18, 136-37, thus including Homer in H's criticism. In Diels-Kranz fg A 22 Homer is also rebuked for the sentiment of Achilles at *Il* 18 107, where he wishes that war (the cardinal principle of H's philosophy, fg 80 Diels-Kranz) would disappear: Guthrie, p. 447; Kirk, pp. 242-43.
12. Plutarch *De Musica* 1132e-1134e (*FHG* 23).
13. Schol Pindar *Ol* 9.1; Pfeiffer, p. 162.
14. E. Fraenkel, note on Aeschylus *Ag* 276.
15. Blumenthal, p. 3.

16. Cratinus fg 131 (Edmonds) (130 K) in his *Nomoi*.

17. Cratinus fg 198 (Edmonds) also parodies a line of Archilochus.

18. Fg 8 T (6D, 13 L/B); Whitman 39.

19. Kirchner I 580 (8880); most of our information about him comes from Aristophanes' abusive comments in several plays.

20. Aristophanes *Peace* 1298 ff.

21. Cratinus fg 1 ff (Edmonds): the 'Archilochoi' possibly refers to a comic plot about Archilochus and his friends. For Archilochus in later comedy see Edmonds vols. 2, 2a and 2b where the references are indexed.

22. Aelian *Var Hist* 10.13. (88 B 44 Diels-Kranz)

23. Solon fg 1, 3-8D. Plato *Republic* 332d (as put forward by 'Polemarchus'); E. Schwarz, *Ethik der Griechen* (Stuttgart 1951), p. 60.

24. Semerano, p. 169.

25. Xenophon, *Memorabilia Socratis* 1, 2, 37; Semerano, p. 169; Guthrie, vol. 3, pp. 178ff; 300-304.

26. E.g. *Republic* 379-388 etc; Grube, chapter 4.

27. Pfeiffer, p. 54.

28. *Ion* 531a-532a; *Republic* 365c.

29. Cope's note on *Rhet* B 23.ii, 1398 b 11, mentions Sauppe's attribution of this passage to the *Mouseion* of Alcidamas; for his writings in general see Blass, vol. 2, pp. 345 ff; L. Radermacher, *Artium Scriptores* (Vienna 1951), pp. 132 ff.; Brzoska, *RE*, s.v. 'Alkidamas'; Guthrie, vol. 3, pp. 311 ff.

30. Kontoleon, op. cit. (notes 9 and 10 above).

31. G. A. Privitera, 'Archiloco e la divinità dell' Archilocheion', *RFIC* 44 (1965) 5-25; Kontoleon; also E. Vanderpool, *AJP* 76 (1955) 186-88.

32. Kontoleon; Privitera, op. cit.; *Mnes. Inscr.* E 1 col III 35-37.

33. Kirchner, vol. 1, pp. 592-93 (8792); Guthrie, vol. 3, pp. 178 ff.; 300-304.

34. Guthrie, vol. 2, p. 159: in Alcidamas' famous speech to the Spartans, encouraging them to release the Messenians from centuries of serfdom.

35. *Mnes. Inscr.* E 1 col II 22-44; Kontoleon, op. cit.; M. L. West, *CR* 14 (1962) 141-42.

36. He mentions and quotes him at: *Rhet* 223 (1398b ii): 317 (1418 b 28) Pol 7, (5), 7 (13228a3); fg 1584a7 (Bonitz); see note 4 above.

37. *Index Operum:* Heraclides Ponticus quoted by Diogenes Laetius 5, 87.

38. Just as he used Solon's poetry for his discussion of the constitution of Athens, *Atheniensium Respublica*, edit. F. G. Kenyon (Oxford Classical Texts 1920): 5.2,3; 6.1,2 and many other places noted in Kenyon's *Index Nominum*; Blumenthal, p. 14.

39. See F. Susemihl's note ad loc *The Politics of Aristotle*, Books 1-4, translated by R. D. Hicks, (London 1895), pp. 501 f.

40. Dio Chrysostomus, *Orat. Tarsica* I, p. 100 (von Arnim).

41. 'Σὺ γὰρ δὴ παρὰ φίλων ἀπάγχεαι' fg 106T (67 6 D; 119 L/B).

42. Athenaeus 451 d: Pfeiffer, p. 146.

43. *Callimachus* edit. (Oxford vol. 1 1949, vol. 2 1953) fgs 380, 544 et al.

44. Athenaeus 85e.

45. Clemens Alexandrinus *Strom* 1, 21, 117.

46. D. A. Russell's discussion on Longinus, pp. xxiii-xxx, sums up the problem of chronology and authorship; there would appear still to be strong reasons for accepting first century A.D.

47. At 10.7; 13.3; 33.5 he seems to appreciate Archilochus' power and vitality of invention.

48. Russell, pp. xxx-xxxiii.

49. Philodemus, *de poem* 2 fgs 1, 28, 29; 4 fg 4; *Pap Herc* 1074, col 105; *Pap Herc* 407, fr 2; *Pap Herc* 446 fg 2 quoted by Tarditi, pp. 41-43; Schmid-Stählin, vol. 1, p. 396; Semerano, p. 169; Grube, pp. 195ff.

50. If, indeed, this is a possible interpretation of *Pap Herc* 207 col 4, Tarditi, p. 41.

51. Quintilian 10, 1, 60: 'summa in hoc (Archilocho) vis elocutionis, cum validae tum breves vibrantesque sententiae, plurimum sanguinis atque nervorum, adeo ut videatur quibusdam, quod quodam minor est, materiae esse non ingenii vitium.'

52. Hauvette, p. 201; Blumenthal, pp. 54-55.

53. *Praep. Ev.* 32 (Migne xxi).

54. φαλάκρας ἐγκώμιον 75 b refers to him as the finest of poets (ὁ κάλλιστος ποιητῶν 'Αρχίλοχος).

55. Synesius ep 130 (on fg 2D 2T 7L/B): Blumenthal considers that S's reference indicates that much of A's poetry continued to be known in the fifth century A.D.

56. Plutarch *Cato* 762; Semerano p. 170.

57. Poem 40 seems to echo A's epode (166T 88D 159L/B); Poems 8 and 42.

58. E. Fraenkel, *Horace* (Oxford 1957), chapter 2 esp pp. 48, 60.

59. On poems 8 and 16: E. Fraenkel, 'Two Poems of Catullus', *JRS* 51 (1961) 46-53; F. W. Lintott, *Violence in Republican Rome* (Oxford 1968), p. 819.

60. F. Lasserre, *Les Épodes d'Archiloque* (Paris 1950); see J. A. Davison's admiring but cautious review in *CR* (1952) 18-19.

61. 118 T.

62. Krumbacher, pp. 281 ff. for the survival of ancient literature, including poetry of Archilochus, Sappho, etc. In the eleventh century Psellos was able to refer to A and others in his funeral oration for his mother: 504 ff. Again it is impossible to determine his firsthand acquaintance with A's poetry.

63. The other source for this fragment is Aelian *Var Hist* 4.14.

64. On the question of anthologies: Krumbacher, pp. 727 ff; J. Barns, *CQ* 44 (1950) 126-137; 45 (1951) 1-19.

65. A. W. Gouldner, *Enter Plato* (London 1965), pp. 12 ff.

CHAPTER 2

1. Pausanias X 28,8; Eusebius *Praep. Ev.* V 17; Stephanus Byzantius, s.v. Thasos.

2. Zeller, I, ii, pp. 1329 f. Kritias: *RE* (Diehl); Nestle, 'Kritias'; Blass vol. 1, pp. 265 ff.; Kirchner, 8729; Diels-Kranz, Kritias.

3. I have deliberately emphasized the abusive elements in my translation in order to give words like μοιχός, λάγνος, ὑβριστής their full tones of acerbity.

4. Diels-Kranz, B 30 ff; Nestle, pp. 181 ff.

5. Diels-Kranz, B 6 f: there may be a pun involved in ἔμμετροι πολιτεῖαι whereby they are both 'well-balanced' and 'versified' (two possible meanings of the adjective).

6. See note 26, chapter 1.

7. The *Republic* as a whole goes far beyond the boundaries of the genre πολιτεῖα (politeia) as exemplified in (Xenophon's) *Athenian Constitution* (the 'Old Oligarch') or the *Respublica Lacedaemoniorum* ascribed to Xenophon, but attributed to Antisthenes by K. M. Atkinson, in *Publications Faculty of Arts Univ Manchester* 1 (1948).

8. Nestle, p. 82; Wilamowitz, *Platon* vol. 1, pp. 116 ff.; Guthrie, vol. 3, pp. 299 f.

9. Guthrie, vol. 3, p. 304.

10. Diels-Kranz, fgs B, 6, 7, 8, (his Constitution of the Lacedaemonians in verse).

11. Philostratus *Vit. Soph.* i. 16.

12. Xenophon *Mem. Socr.* 1, 2. 12ff.

13. Diels-Kranz, fg B 1.

14. Wilamowitz, *Sappho und Simonides* (Dublin/Stuttgart 1960), p. 180.

15. G. Tarditi, *PP*, p. 124.

16. See note 29, chapter 1; Aristotle *Rhet.* 1398 b 11; that it probably was a tradition of some age and standing is perhaps indicated by the perfect tense in which the reference is couched.

17. Jacoby, p. 97 n. 4, seems to imply a biographical sequence in Critias' notice.

18. Diels-Kranz, B fg 9; Guthrie, vol. 3, p. 256.

19. Guthrie, vol. 3, p. 69 (ref Diels-Kranz, fg 69).

20. See Diels- Kranz, vol. 2, Antiphon, also the summary of his views; Guthrie, vol. 3, pp. 108 ff.

21. Gouldner, pp. 81-90; E. R. Dodds, *The Greek and the Irrational* (California 1951).

22. Guthrie, vol. 3, p. 299, n. 1.

23. Socrates' blunt rebuke was provoked by Critias' insistent attempts to seduce Euthydemus: Xenophon *Mem. Socr.* 1, 2, 12 ff (Diels-Kranz, fg A 4).

24. C. Gallavotti, pp. 130-53; Tarditi, *PP*, 122-39; S. Luria, *Philologus* 105 (1961) 178-91; W. Donlan, *Historia* 22 (1973) 145-54.

25. Tarditi, *PP*, p. 126.

26. Pindar *Pyth.* 2, 53-58.

27. Schol ad Pindar *Pyth.* 2, 99-101.

28. Both meanings are found in Plato: (a) as meaning lack of means in *Republic* 405b and *Laws* 830b; (b) meaning impasse in thought or decision in *Prot* 324d, *Gorg* 522a, *Phaed* 108c, et al.

29. Oenomaus quoted by Eusebius *Praep. Ev.* 6, 7, 8.

30. Possibly in a poem of similar flavour to *Pap Ox* 2310 (54 T 35 L/B) since this is the expression of a man asserting faith in his own future prospects, in spite of adverse appearances.

31. Eusebius 5, 31.1; Parke and Wormell, vol. 2, *The Oracular Responses*, p. 95; Poem 54 T (see note 29 above) seems to imply an invitation (from the same source) to Archilochus to go and take up the leadership of the colony on Thasos.

32. For various non-sexual connotations of the word: K. J. Dover, *Greek Popular Morality in the Time of Plato and Aristotle* (Oxford 1974), pp. 54 f.

33. Merkelbach and West, pp. 97-113.

34. K. J. Dover, *Arethusa* 6, 1 (1973) 59.

35. Dover, op. cit., rejects distinction between the 'magical' licence of Old Comedy and the iambicists and painters of pottery.

36. Aristophanes *Ranae* 1044; cf. Plato *Republic* 395d, who prohibits the representation of the ἐρῶσα γυνή in poetry.

37. The tradition is supported by *Hom. Hymn* 5, 195, but it can only be regarded as representing reasonable but unestablished hypothesis: Schmid-Stählin, pp. 387 ff; T. S. Duncan, *WUS* 7 (1920) 19-37; Gallavotti; Tarditi, *PP*; F. Will, *CJ* (1961) 289-96.

38. Diels-Kranz, Critias.

39. 8 T (6 D 13 L/B).

40. 96 T (60 D 93 L/B); Rankin, *Hermathena*, p. 91.

41. *Odyssey* 19, 359 (see note 24 above).

42. Duncan, op. cit. (note 37), p. 20; Gallavotti, p. 140.

43. 54 T; vv 12-13, 'Did I seem to be a man of no account and not of such a quality as I am: and not of such kindred?' Also Rankin, *Eranos* (1974), p. 5.

44. 80 T (L/B 57); 81 T (L/B 58).

45. 54 T: Rankin, *Eranos* (1974), pp. 5-7.

46. Teucer is undoubtedly secondary in status and power of character to Aias in Sophocles' play: see W. B. Stanford, *Sophocles' Ajax* (London 1963), p. xlviii. It is difficult to decide the date of this play with any certainty, but it is certainly some years after Pericles' legislation on the parental qualifications for citizenship: Stanford, Appendix G.

47. *Mnes. Inscr.* E, col II 50-51: the oracle says that Telesicles' son who first meets him as he steps ashore will be 'immortal' and famous amongst mankind in song. If it were supposed that there were only one son, there would hardly be any need to specify him in this way— even in a latterly concocted myth! Parke and Wormell, vol. 2, p. 95, accept the implication that T. had more than one son.

48. Ἀρχίλοχ' εἰς Θάσον ἐλθέ καὶ οἴκει εὔκλεα νῆσον: Oenomaus quoted by Eusebius in *Praep. Ev.* 5, 31. 'Archilochus, go to Thasos and settle (in) the famous island.' The imperative

οἴκει could mean 'settle' or 'colonize' or 'administer/rule'. For a similar idea in the poet's own mind: T 54 (Pap. Ox. 2310) 16-20, where he seems to envisage himself called to be ruler of a πόλις, probably Thasos. The motive of A's going to Thasos would appear to be poverty as a result of misjudged political disbursements, according to Oenomaus' introductory remarks. Critias similarly represents poverty as his motive.

49. Plutarch *de poet aud.* 33 a-b.
50. Gallavotti, p. 140; Rankin, *Symbolae Osloenses*, pp. 45-46.
51. Herodotus 3, 39, 139-40; Pape-Benseler, vol. 2, p. 1456.
52. W. B. Stanford, *The Odyssey of Homer, edited with general and grammatical introduction, commentary, etc.* (London 1947), pp. xxi f.; for significant names upon which conscious play is made: O. Lendle, *Die Pandorasage bei Hesiod* (Würtzburg 1957), pp. 117 ff.
53. *Odyssey* 1.62: Athene's words: 'τί νύ οἱ τόσον ὠδύσαο, Ζεῦ;' 'Why then were you so angry with him, Zeus?' See also Stanford's note ad loc.
54. 16 T.
55. 110 T.
56. H. W. Parke, *Greek Mercenary Soldiers* (Oxford 1931), p. 4, accepts the tradition as probably valid; Gallavotti, p. 137 is sceptical.
57. See note 49 above.
58. 1 T.
59. See notes 48 and 49 above.
60. Kontoleon, *Arkh. Eph.*, p. 56; M. L. West, *CR* 14, 141-42 (see chapter 1 note 35).
61. F. Dornseiff, *Theologische Literaturzeitung* 7/8 (1955) 499-500.
62. W. Peek, *Philologus* 99 (1955) 1-50.
63. For a full discussion of ancient examples of such encounters, see A. Kambylis, 'Zur Dichterweihe des Arkhilochos', *Hermes* 101 (1963) 129-50 (particularly pp. 133-40); also Kontoleon, *Entretiens*, p. 48.
64. Tarditi *PP*, p. 122 discusses evidence for strong Delphic influence in the *Archilocheion*.
65. Parke and Wormell, vol. 2, p. 170.
66. Kambylis (op. cit. note 63), p. 131-32, suggests that Telesicles consulted the oracle on the very question of his son, the cow and the lyre. If so, he probably used the opportunity of his public mission to Delphi to put this extra question on his own personal behalf.
67. See chapter 1 note 32.
68. Kontoleon, *Arkh. Eph.*, p. 80.
69. For the theory of strong Delphic 'propagandist' influence in the *Mnes. Inscr.* account, see Tarditi *PP*, p. 122.
70. (Oenomaus) Eusebius *Praep. Ev.* 32; Heraclides Ponticus *Pol.* 8.
71. Suda s.v. Arkhilokhos; Eusebius loc. cit.
72. Parke, p. 94.
73. *Mnes. Inscr.* E, col II. The Muses (naturally) and Zeus, Athene, Poseidon, Heracles, Dionysus, Artemis.
74. The word *iambos* first occurs in fg 20 T, in which it is plainly contrasted with poems of eulogy; and Schmid-Stählin, 1 i, p. 386; *RE* (Gerhard) s.v., Aristotle *Poetic* 1448 b 32; on which see Bywater's note, *Aristotle on the Art of Poetry* (Oxford 1909), pp. 130-31; Lesky, p. 110. It is reasonable conjecture that Archilochus' family was connected with the cult of Demeter: N. J. Richardson, *The Homeric Hymn to Demeter* (Oxford 1974), pp. 213 f.; the iambus and its attendant *aischrologia* was closely associated with her worship. The evidence of Pausanias X 28 is interesting but inconclusive; it seems clear, however, that Delphi and Apollo had a special interest in the poet.
75. 165 T; 205 T; Pouilloux, *Entretiens*, p. 19.
76. Pausanias X 28; J. G. Frazer, *Pausanias' Description of Greece*, vol. 5 (London 1913), pp. 373 ff.
77. *RE* s.v. Tellis (W. Göber).
78. Ibid.

79. Ibid.

80. See note 64 above.

81. H. J. Mette, *Hermes* 88 (1960) 493-94.

82. Aphrodite 149 T; Apollo 30 T; Ares 3 T, 31 T, 98 T, 188 T (Enyalios 1 T); Athene 4 T, 121 T, 126 T; Demeter 165 T, 205 T; Dionysus 117 T; Hephaistos 12 T, 115 T; Heracles 207 T; Hermes (?) 122 T; Kore 205 T; Muses 1 T; Poseidon 14 T, 211 T; Zeus 51 T, 55 T, 107 T, 114 T, 121 T, 126 T, 145 T, 148 T, 174 T, 220 T. Little can be deduced from this selection except the not unexpected preponderance of Zeus.

83. By whom, however, he was strongly influenced in his art: V. Steffen, *Eos* 46 (1952–53) 33-48; T. Breitenstein 'Hésiode et Archiloque', *Odense University Classical Studies* 1 (1971).

84. For references, note 145 below.

85. These happen to occur in iambics, tetrameters, and epodic poems, but not in elegiacs (but this may be fortuitous).

86. If we compare the number of references to the Lycambids with the number of references to named individuals in the surviving fragments we obtain a proportion of 6 ± 2/20 ± 3 allowing for doubtful cases. This is a very rough estimate (based on Tarditi's index); since there are probably many other references to the Lyc. and to distinct individuals other than Lyc. which are concealed from us by the very nature of the fragments. Our fragments as we possess them hardly constitute a random sample of A's verses, in that their original inclusion as quotations in literature often indicates that they were worth choosing for some illustrative purpose. Reference to persons and personal characteristics probably was a factor in the choice of many of them.

87. Horace *Epodes* 6, 11; *Epist.* 1, 19, 23; (schol on Horace *Epodes* 6, 13) are the earliest and most significant, considering Horace's careful study of Archilochus as a model for his *Epodes*.

88. According to Lasserre's reconstruction of line 27 of *Pap Ox* 2310 (not accepted by Tarditi 54 T). There is a clear reference to Neoboule as a potential spouse of A in the *Col Pap* poem, 15-17.

89. 166 T.

90. 111 T; Broccia, p. 21.

91. 241 T, 244 T, 258 T. The insults μυσάχνη 258 T; δῆμος 241 T; ἐργάτις 244 T, may possibly characterize Neoboule as a prostitute; A's hostility to her is quite openly expressed in *Col Pap* 15-25; and in the tradition of Hellenistic epigram, e.g. Dioscorides *AP* 7, 351; Iul. Aegypt. *AP* 7, 69; 7, 70; also Bond, pp. 1-11.

92. 54 T, *Pap. Ox.* 2310, 15-20.

93. 24 T: παῖδα τὴν ὑπερτέρην, usually taken as meaning the 'younger' daughter, as indicated by the schol on *Iliad* 11 (Λ) 796, in Venetus A.

94. Note 92 above; Dioscorides' epigram envisages a response on behalf of both sisters to the charges A has made against their moral characters.

95. Possibly fgs 25-27 T which describe feminine beauty refer to Neoboule (Synesius, however, regards 25 as applied to a whore): for a discussion see Marzullo.

96. S. Luria, *Philologus* 105 (1961) 178-197 (p. 180).

97. *Mnes. Inscr.* E. 1, col 45.

98. *Col Pap* 7: Merkelbach and West, p. 104; Marcovich, p. 8. This poem will be discussed at greater length in chapter 5; on the queston of its authenticity, see Appendix.

99. Merkelbach and West; Marcovich suggests that the reference to Amphimedo is merely a formal compliment. This praise of the beauty of a beauty's mother is a traditional lyric motive echoed by Horace *Odes* 1, 16, 1, *O matre pulchra filia pulchrior*.

100. J. M. Edmonds, *PCPhS* (1930) 6-7; *Elegy and Iambus*, vol. 2 (Loeb Series, London 1961) pp. 315-322.

101. J. Pouilloux, 'Glaucos fils de Leptine, Parien', *BCH* 79 (1955) 75-86; cf. J. and L. Robert, *REG* (69) 1956, 154-56.

102. 15 T, 6 L/B; 91 T, 103 L/B; 95 T, 92 L/B.
103. Tarditi, *RFIC*, p. 113.
104. Cicero, *Tusc. Disp.* 1, 1.3, places him in the age of Romulus; for an earlier dating than that of the 'consensus' mentioned in the text: E. Blakeway, 'The Date of Archilochus', *Greek Poetry and Life* (Oxford 1936) 34-55; and a later: E. Loewy, *AAWW* 70 (1933) 31-34.
105. Pouilloux, *Entretiens* 10 (1964) 1-36, p. 16; Robert, op. cit. (note 101).
106. Jacoby, *FGH* II 239: 24-30 (Marmor Parium 33).
107. Pouilloux, op. cit. (note 105).
108: 3 D, 9 L/B.
109. Plutarch *Theseus* 2f-3a; *RE* s.v. Abantes (Toepfer).
110. Thucydides 1, 15, 3; cf. Herodotus 5, 49.10.
111. A. W. Gomme, *A Historical Commentary on Thucydides*, vol. 1 (Oxford 1945) p. 126; Donlan, p. 139.
112. Plutarch *Mor* 153 f; W. G. Forrest, *Historia* 6 (1957) 160-175 (p. 160).
113. Forrest, p. 164; Jacoby, *CQ*, p. 108.
114. Donlan, p. 139.
115. Aulus Gellius 17, 21, 8; Jacoby *Apollodors*, p. 142.
116. Herodotus 1.12; Jacoby, *CQ*, p. 97.
117. Herodotus 1.12: A. H. Sayce's note on this passage: *The Ancient Empires of the East, Herodotus* I-III (London 1883) is still useful. There would appear to be no reason to deny the authenticity of the passage.
118. 22 T.
119. Tarditi, *RFIC*, p. 113.
120. Jacoby *Apollodors*, p. 142.
121. Jacoby *CQ*, pp. 106-7.
122. 19 T.
123. Jacoby *CQ*, p. 106; Tarditi *RFIC*, p. 114.
124. Jacoby *CQ*, p. 104.
125. Jacoby *CQ,* p. 107.
126. K. J. Dover, *Entretiens*, pp. 201 ff.
127. 114 T; 82 L/B; *Pap. Ox.* (1954) 2313.
128. E. Dutoit, *Le Thème de l'Adynaton dans la poésie antique* (Paris 1936), p. 4.
129. Jacoby *CQ*, p. 97 mentions 648 (or 647) B.C. as the date and thereafter refers to the year as 648. I prefer to follow Oppolzer and Newton, pp. 91-94; in referring to it as 647 B.C.
130. Newton pp. 91-94, regards these two as statistically no more improbable than the others.
131. See Oppolzer, op. cit.
132. See Newton, pp. 91-94.
133. See Fotheringham, pp. 104-126.
134. Ibid., p. 108.
135. Newton, p. 93; L. Motz and A. Duveen, *Essentials of Astronomy* (London 1966), pp. 5, 6.
136. Ibid., p. 93.
137. Ibid., pp. 91-94.
138. Oppolzer, p. 27: this diagram actually shows the eclipse of 656 B.C. Achieving totality in the required region: cf. Hauvette, pp. 11-14.
139. Jacoby *Apollodors*, p. 150; in *CQ* he suggests (p. 101) that this date was chosen for the *floruit* because it was the last year of Gyges according to the old computation of his reign (rendered obsolete by Gelzer *RhM* 30 [1875]), and sometimes the *floruit* of a famous man was associated with a fixed event in the life of some prominent personage such as a king.
140. Lacey, pp. 106-7; G. H. Polman, *CP* LXIX 3 (1974) 169-77.
141. See note 126 above.
142. Approximately; in view of the differences in year calculation between antiquity and ourselves.

143. Note 126: even older, perhaps. Even on the assumption of a quick poetic reaction to an infuriating event, there would be some interval before the work was composed; i.e. the technical problem of completing a poem, not the time needed for 'emotion to be recollected in tranquility', etc.

144. Lacey, p. 71: Hesiod *Works and Days* 695-701.

145. Lycambes: 24 T; 67, 2 T; 73, 166 T; Neoboule 111 T; probably 54 T also, and the Cologne fragment.

146. The device is a very common one. It is not immediately apparent which passages of *Philippus* Aristotle means but the reference in Antidosis is clear enough: see Cope's commentary notes.

147. See L/B note on L/B 82 (p. 27) (114 T); Lasserre *Museum Helveticum* 4 (1947) 1 ff.

148. 10 T; 20 T.

149. For meanings and association of ψόγος 'ψέγει', see Bywater's note on Aristotle *Poet* 1448b 32 (note 71 above) (and on 1448b 28 where ψόγοι are contrasted with 'praises' (ἐπαινοί): also *Rhet* 1358f 13): there seems to be an implication of 'public' as distinct from merely 'private' blame. Simonides fg I Ar *Eth N* 1100 f 22): Pindar *Pyth* II 100 specifically calls Archilochus ψογερόν; also Sophocles *Ant* 759; Euripides *Bacch* 778: 'fearful at the blame of fellow citizens, etc', Plato, *Gorg* 483c 'ψόγους ψέγουσι'.

150. *Index Hesych Aristot*, cf. chapter 1 notes 3 and 35.

151. For a different interpretation, see Dover, *Entretiens*, pp. 206-7.

152. 10 T.

153. 166 T; we cannot completely discount the possibility that Aristotle, well acquainted though he was with Archilochus' poetry, did not know who the people were who were mentioned in this poem, since his work on Archilochus was entitled ἀπορήματα, 'puzzles' or 'difficulties'.

154. Cf. Dover, p. 207.

155. 7 T, 8 T, 87 T.

156. 8 T, 47 T, 91 T, 92 T; see also F. J. Cuartero, *BIEH* 11, 2 (1968) 41-45.

157. 18 T.

158. 5 T.

159. Plutarch *Inst. Lac.* 239 b.

160. 18 T: 'the place is not in any way beautiful, or desirable, nor attractive, as (in the land) around the waters of Siris.'

161. 17 T.

162. 91 T.

163. D'A. W. Thompson, *CR* (1941) 67; F. H. Sandbach, *CR* (1942) 63-65; Steffen, *Eos* 47 (1954) 51-62 (p. 61); Cuartero, op. cit. (note 156).

164. 2 T; 54 T, but there are indications *passim* in the surviving verses; the fluidity of his attitude and his disregard of convention suggest not only a man of independent character; but also one who was not constrained to live indefinitely under the pressure of hostile opinion: 9 T, he advises disregard of public opinion.

165. 16 T; 95 T; see chapter 3.

166. Homer *Il* 2 530 distinguished *Panhellenes* from *Akhaioi*: the distinction is not absolutely clear-cut and the line has been suspected (probably without justification); Hesiod, *Works and Days* 528, and Archilochus 88 T, are the first to use Panhellenes of all the Greeks as distinct from those of the North, according to Apollodorus (fg 200 Jacoby): see Tarditi's note on fg 88 T.

167. ὀϊζύς.

168. Schol Ovid *Ibis*, p. 521.

169. See notes 70, 71 above.

170. But not at all likely: see Jacoby's comments in *CQ*, p. 107, note 4.

171. For background and examples of this, E. Kretschmer, *Psychology of Men of Genius*, translated by Cattell (London 1931); H. C. Lehmann, *Age and Achievement* (Princeton 1953).

172. Heraclides Ponticus *Pol.* 8. See chapter 1 note 22.

173. See note 72 above.

174. F. Will, *Archilochus (Twaynes World Author Series* 59, New York 1960), p. 17.

175. Cherniss, pp. 15-30.

176. Ibid., p. 25.

177. Ibid., p. 15.

178. Similarly Sophocles' account of his relief at being in his old age no longer subject to sexual desire (Plato *Republic* 329 c; Plutarch 525 a) adds to our understanding of his study of old age in *Oedipus at Colonus.*

179. Cherniss, pp. 21-22.

180. K. Quinn, *Ramus* 1.2 (1972) 91-101 (pp. 92-3).

181. Cherniss, p. 29.

182. Although there are marked indications of oral poetic techniques in the fragments; D. L. Page, *Entretiens*, pp. 119-165, the question here is of their 'public tone' even in the discussion of private subjects.

CHAPTER 3

1. *AP* 7, 674.

2. See chapter 1 note 5: (*De Sublimitate* 13 3).

3. See chapter 1 notes 7, 8, 9, 12, 15.

4. See chapter 2 note 83.

5. H. Langerbeck marshals evidence and arguments which suggest that the *Margites* was regarded as of considerable importance and of ancient origin: *HSCP* 72 (1958) 33-62. D. L. Page 'Archilochus and the Oral Tradition', *Entretiens*, p. 146, seems to accept Eustratius' statement that Archilochus mentioned the *Margites.* Others are somewhat sceptical especially on account of the lateness (12th century A.D.) of Eustratius. He tells us that Cratinus (cf. chapter 1 note 21) and Archilochus regarded the *Margites* as 'Homeric'. The least drastic emendation, that of Bergk, (Ἀρχιλόχοις for Ἀρχίλοχος) would suggest that Cratinus in 5th century B.C. had some reason to believe that Archilochus was interested in *Margites* and mentioned this in a play, *Arkhilokhoi.* See J. A. Davison's cautious discussion: *Eranos* 53 (1955) 125-139 (particularly 134-5). On the whole it seems reasonable to suppose that *Margites*, or something like it, antedated Archilochus.

6. The use of words like 'literary' and 'literature' of an art which does not use, or does not depend upon writing, only seems paradoxical because of the etymology of these words in English (and some other languages); see René Wellek and Austin Warren, *Theory of Literature* (London 1949), pp. 22-23.

7. See chapter 2 notes 37, 74.

8. Crusius *RE* article: Archilochos; Treu; B. Snell, *Antike* (1941) 5-34; S. Gerevini, *PP* 9 (1954) 256-64; Davison, op. cit. (note 5); G. Setti 'Omero ed Archiloco', *RSA* 2 fasc 4, 101-113; on the predominence of epic words in A's vocabularly: U Bahnjte, *Quaestiones Archilocheae*, Diss. Inaug. Göttingen 1900: A. Hauvette, 236; G. C. Motta, *RIL* 96 (1962) 550-64; Page, *Entretiens*, pp. 119-63.

9. See chapter 2 note 21.

10. Milman Parry's original definition of epic *formula* was 'a group of words which is regularly employed with the same metrical conditions to express a given essential idea'. 'The Traditional Epithet in Homer', as reprinted in Parry, p. 13.

11. The question of the degree of flexibility admitted in the notion of the formula, before the poetry ceases to be properly describable as 'formulaic' in character, has and still does exercise those who study the *epos*; for a resumé of the various 'schools' and other opinions see Parry, op. cit., p. xxxiii.

12. 'The Homeric Gloss. A study in Word-Sense', Parry, pp. 140-50; see also D. L. Page, 'The Laestrygonians', in *Folktales in Homer's Odyssey,' The Carl Newell Jackson Lectures* (Cambridge Mass. 1972), pp. 33-38.

13. For a forceful, if lengthy, exposition of this obvious point: D. C. Young, 'Never Blotted a Line? Formula and Premeditation in Homer and Hesiod', *Arion* 3 (1967) 279-324.

14. J. B. Hainsworth, *The Flexibility of the Homeric Formula* (Oxford 1968), pp. 2-3.

15. G. P. Edwards, *The Language of Hesiod in Its Traditional Context* (Oxford 1971), pp. 50-54; A. Hoekstra, *The Sub-Epic Stage of the Formulaic Tradition, Studies in the Homeric Hymns to Apollo, to Aphrodite and to Demeter* (Amsterdam/London 1969).

16. Page, *Entretiens*, pp. 119-136.

17. Ibid., pp. 137.

18. Ibid., p. 160.

19. L. H. Jeffrey, *The Local Scripts of Archaic Greece* (Oxford 1961), pp. 56-58, points out that there is no positive evidence of papyrus being available in Greece in the Archaic period; but mentions the possible use of skins and leather to write on (as in ἀχνυμένη σκυτάλη). Page (p. 162 opposes the view that leather was a likely writing material, on the grounds that this phrase of A quoted in support of it remains obscure.

20. 188 T.

21. Pfeiffer, p. 220.

22. Dover, *Entretiens*, p. 164.

23. J. Stallworthy, *Between the Lines: Yeats' Poetry in the Making* (Oxford 1962); *Vision and Revision* (Oxford 1969).

24. W. B. Yeats, *Autobiographies* (London 1955): 'The Bounty of Sweden', pp. 532 f; describes how he begins to 'talk to himself' dramatizing himself in various personae, and 'occasionally I write out what I have said in verse, and generally for no better reason than because I remember that I have written no verse for a long time—when I begin to write I have no object but to find for them (the soliloquies) some natural speech, rhythm and syntax and to set it out in some pattern'. Even though writing plays a part here, the poet's composition is primarily oral, and aural; Oliver St. John Gogarty, *W. B. Yeats, A Memoir* (Dublin 1943), p. 23, mentions the poet 'humming and murmuring to himself, and jotting the verse down'.

25. F. Berry, *Poet's Voices* (London 1962), pp. 181-2; A. Dougherty, *A Study of Rhythmic Structure in the Verse of W. B. Yeats* (The Hague 1973), esp. 10-11.

26. In this connection and that of the preceding discussion, it is perhaps helpful to recall that writing, even when a people have it, is not necessarily used by them for literary purposes, see H. M and N. K. Chadwick, *The Growth of Literature*, vol. 3 (Cambridge (1940) p. 697.

27. Plato *Phaedrus* 274 B-278 B.

28. Even in the fifth century B.C., when papyrus was readily available, it was an expensive commodity; Jeffrey, p. 57.

29. It has been newly written on tablets (δέλτοι) and the poet asks the Muses to come down from Helicon into his heart 'for the sake of' this already written ἀοιδή (*Batrachomyomachia* 1-3); he is asking them to inspire his 'recital' rather than his original creation of the poem, an invocation characteristic enough of the ῥαψῳδός. The poem is no doubt the production of an age in which writing was normally involved to some degree in the composition and recording of poetry; but these lines represent a vestigial expression of a traditional attitude which did not invariably and sharply distinguish creation of a work from its performance.

30. Notopoulos, p. 181.

31. A. Hoekstra, *Homeric Modifications of Formulaic Prototypes, Studies in the Development of Greek Epic Diction* (Amsterdam/London 1969), pp. 16-17.

32. Notopoulos, p. 194; Page, *Entretiens*, p. 120.

33. 'Homer' is here used as a term of convenience, without prejudice as to whether it represents a group or an individual, but regarding it as connotative of the *Iliad, Odyssey* and their accompanying tradition, attributions and associations in the ancient world.

34. Gallavotti, p. 132.

35. T. Schlonsky, 'Literary Parody, Remarks on its Method and Function', *Proc IVth Congress of the International Comparative Literature Assoc.* (Paris 1966), pp. 797-801.

36. F. W. Householder, *CP* 39 (1944) 1-9 (esp p. 2); Schmid-Stählin 1.1.401; the fundamental reference to H is Aristotle *Poetic* 1448a 12.

37. Schmid-Stählin 1.1.401.

38. V. Mercier, *The Irish Comic Tradition* (Oxford 1962), pp. 3-4, on the theory that parody is one of the later developments of literary humour, coming after more primitive traits such as word-play.

39. For parodies of the *Odyssey* in the *mimos*, fgs 14, 50; A. Olivieri, *Frammenti della commedia greca e del mimo nella Sicilia e nella Magna Grecia* (Naples 1930).

40. Hipponax 77 D Masson 128: Μοῦσα μοι Εὐρυμεδοντιάδεω τὴν ποντοχάρυβδιν, τὴν ἐγγαστριμάχαιραν, ὃς ἐσθίει οὐ κατὰ κόσμον κτλ.

41. *Odyssey* 6 196, 9-20; 20 18; Gallavotti, p. 133; H. Harder, *Hermes* 80 (1952) 381-4; M. Gigante, *PP* 12 (1957) 360-62; (cf. G. Morelli, *Maia* 1 [1948] 104-7).

42. Page, *Entretiens* p. 136, rejects this line as a later forgery. He points out that εὐήθης does not appear in Greek at this period. While its occurrence at such an early period, unsupported by contemporary parallels, is suspicious, it is hardly feasible to deny the possibility of its existence in A's period. Our knowledge of the resources of vocabulary in 7th century b.c. is very scanty, because we have so little Greek of that century remaining. Nor can I agree with him that the couplet gives the impression of a Hellenistic epigram, 'the work of a studious composer pen in hand'.

43. The word δέκτρια, with its cognate verb δέχομαι ('receive') seems to have a sexual connotation: D. E. Gerber, *QUCC* (1973) 105-109 (esp. pp. 108-109).

44. Chapter 2 notes 50-54.

45. See H. J. Mette's discussion, *Hermes* 88 (1960) 493-94.

46. Page, *Entretiens* pp. 127-8, compares the movement of the elegy fr 7 D (10 T) with that of *Iliad* 12, 310 ff (statement of case; philosophical reflection; exhortation); but his interesting analysis does not prove, as he implies, that the fg of A. is substantially a formal piece of technical construction which as a whole 'could stand in just these words and phrases, in a speech by a person in the *Iliad*'. Archilochus' consolation to Pericles has solemnity and power blended with personal feeling; and it achieves its effect by means of using the traditional diction with a particular intention and for an individual purpose.

47. This line, quoted here as it appears in some of the authors who quote the fragment, has in it the fine epic phrase, θανάτου τέλος (cf. *Iliad* 3 309, *Odyssey* 5 326). Aristophanes, *Pax* 1298 ff has the variant, ψυχὴν δ'ἐξεσάωσα which implies the completion quoted elsewhere τί μοι μέλει ἀσπὶς ἐκείνη: 'I saved my life, what does that shield matter to me?', a version which with the slight variation of αὐτόν (self) for ψυχήν was followed in the Neoplatonists' quotations. Although it may be the case that Aristophanes altered the text of Archilochus to suit his own purposes and Attic usage (M. Platnauer in *Aristophanes' Peace* [Oxford 1964], note on 1298; M. Gigante, *PP* 40-41 [1955–56] 196-200 [esp p. 199]), it is not unreasonable to suppose that Archilochus' text (and tradition) had variations of considerable antiquity.

48. Gouldner, pp. 12-16.

49. Plutarch *Instit. Lacon.* 34 (239 b); Valerius Maximus 6.3 ext 1 (p. 291 Kenoff) (Tarditi *Archil.*): *Testimonia* 143, 182).

50. Chapter 2 above: also Rankin, *GB*, pp. 323-34.

51. Aristophanes *Pax* 1298 ff.

52. In using the phrase ἐντὸς ἀμώμητον, he is deliberately turning "formula" to his own purpose, a process of adaptation which is continuative of tradition which he criticizes in some of its aspects, but does not reject. See further: Broccia; Gallavotti, p. 134.

53. 102 T.

54. See Schlonsky.

55. Broccia; V. de Falco, *PP* 1 (1946) 347-59; Gallavotti, p. 134; Terzaghi, pp. 23-24.

56. Kirchner, 8880; Aristophanes *Nubes* 353 acuses him of throwing away his shield.

57. Herodotus 5, 95 mentions a similar loss occurring to Alcaeus; Anacreon 85 (Gentili); Horace *Odes* 2, 7, 9-10; Terzaghi, pp. 23-24.

58. 96 T.

59. 'Glaucos, the ἐπίκουρος (mercenary, ally, 38 T) is one's friend so long as he fights', a fg quoted in Aristotle, *Eudemian Ethics* 1236a 33, and attributed to Archilochus by Th. Bergk with great probability.

60. Rankin, *Hermathena*, pp. 91-98.

61. H. Fränkel, *Dichtung*, pp. 186 ff.

62. P. Walcot, *Greek Peasants, Ancient and Modern* (Manchester 1970) p. 70.

63. *Iliad* 1.149 ff.

64. *Iliad* 2.265 ff.

65. Reluctance to seek revenge for dishonour inflicted in an 'honour' (or 'shame') society is well illustrated in R. Vailland's novel 'The Law' (*La Loi*, Paris 1957): translated by P. Wills (London 1958), pp. 61-62: 'He (Don Cesare) used to touch the girls' thighs, in front of their parents, sitting erect in the uncomfortable Venetian chairs; he felt their breasts and buttocks; he appraised, gauged, judged with crude words. The fathers and brothers discreetly left their places and pretended to chat by the window, backs to the room so that their honour did not compel them to intervene. The mothers cried: "Ah, Don Cesare, you don't change a bit. You'll never get old...."'

66. It is possible that there is such an implication in the αἶνός of the fox and the eagle, whether or not the reference is to the injustice done to the poet by the Lycambids: Lassarre, pp. 45-6; Wolf, pp. 50-61.

67. Gerevini, pp. 256-64.

CHAPTER 4

1. Horace *Epode* 6, 11; *Serm.* 2, 3 11; *Epist.* 1, 19, 23; *Ars Poet.* 79 (Tarditi, *Archil.* 84, 85, 86, 87); cf. chapter 2 note 87 above.

2. *Epist.* 1, 19, 31: *nec sponsae laqueum famoso carmine nectit.*

3. *Epist.* 1, 19, 2315: *Parios ego primus iambos ostendi Latio/numeros animosque secutus/Archilochi non res et agentia verba Lycamben.*

4. Ovid *Ibis* 54.

5. However, Ovid's scholiast is positive that Lycambes hanged himself, so also are the scholiasts on the Ovidian passage. The latter is certain of the statement that Archilochus was pursued by the friends of Lycambes, and himself eventually committed suicide—a story for which there is no other evidence whatever. The scholia also contain a disquieting reference to Hipponax, which may be derived from the plot of a comic play in which Archilochus confronts this other great satirist: cf. chapter 2 note 168 above.

6. Gaetulicus, *AP* 7, 71 is our only authority for three rather than two daughters.

7. See note 3 above.

8. E.g., it has a third century B.C. predecessor, the theme of which it follows: Bond, pp. 1-11, see chapter 2 note 91.

9. Eusebius *Praep. Ev.* 5, 32.

10. Another Lycambid, a sister of Neoboule if the Cologne Papyrus is authentic; the fragment *Pap Ox* 2310 is addressed to a woman who very probably is Neoboule, though F. R. Adrados has reservations about this: *PP* 41 (1955–56) 38-48; see also chapter 2 note 88.

11. Nor Hipponax either, nor any other composer of like material: Julian *Epist.* 89 b 300 C.

12. Julian *Misopog.* 1. 337 a.

13. Julian *Epist.* 80.

14. Chapter 2 notes 84, 85.

15. Chapter 2 note 86.
16. *Mnes. Inscr.* E 1, col II, 45.
17. V. Grassmann, *Die Erotischen Epoden des Horaz, Literarischer Hintergrund und Sprachliche Tradition* (Munich 1966), p. 4.
18. In a play of Diphilus (Athenaeus 599 d).
19. Bond, p. 11.
20. See the discussion in chapter 5, also the appendix.
21. Wolf, p. 33.
22. Hauvette, p. 69; Wolf, pp. 62-63.
23. See chapter 2 above.
24. It is impossible to be quite certain of this in view of the brevity of the extract, but the intention of Critias seems to have been to emphasize Archilochus' self-destructive tendencies rather than the analytical one of comprehending all the facts about his relationship with other people. He is propounding a case—as apparently Alcidamas also is—not writing biography.
25. The occurrence of the work ἰαμβικώτερον is probably to be translated as 'rather too satirically' in its context of A's exile: *Mnes. Inscr.* E, col III, 37; Ovid's scholiast on *Ibis* 521 seems to know the story about his exile for satirical acerbity.
26. Bond, p. 11.
27. Fgs 54 T 10-11; 104 T; 109 T.
28. E.g., 30 T, in which he asks Apollo to curse some person or persons, has no apparent connection with the Lycambid family.
29. 193 T.
30. Lasserre, *Les Epodes* etc.
31. 36 T.
32. Piccolomini, pp. 264 ff.; Bond, p. 10 n. 11; M. Treu, pp. 251-52.
33. Piccolomini, pp. 264 ff.; Hauvette, p. 69.
34. 103 T. The phrase follows a Homeric model: *Odyssey* 22, 412, and is also echoed by Cratinus (see Tarditi's comments on the fragment); for a different view, Grassmann, pp. 4-5.
35. The most palpable attack in the fragments themselves is 166 T (see chapter 2 note 91), the epodic fragment beginning πάτερ Λυκάμβα; other fragments less certain nevertheless suggest strongly the reputation of the beauty and virtue of the daughter: Rankin, *GB*. The Cologne Papyrus also is a fierce attack upon Neoboule; for the rest, there is the secondary tradition discussed above.
36. For references to recent articles, etc., propounding this view see Rankin, *Eos*, p. 1; the best known proponents of the 'magic' theory are Hendrickson, pp. 101-27; Elliott, *Power*, pp. 1-15; *Antaios* 4 (1963) 313-26. Also Vendryes, pp. 94-96.
37. Chapter 2 note 74.
38. For an attempted reconstruction of this oracle, see Parke, p. 93.
39. Kontoleon, *Arkh. Eph.* pp. 80 f.; Rankin, *Eos*, footnotes 79-85.
40. 54 T (*Pap Ox* 2310): Rankin, *Eranos*, p. 7.
41. Piccolomini, p. 266.
42. *Iliad* 3, 39; 13, 769, cf. αἰνόπαρις in Alcman fg 40 and other combinations of δυς- and αἰνο- etc. as formulae of abuse.
43. A repetitive element can be seen in the refrain of Theocritus *Idyll* 2, which is about a magic spell; also perhaps in Catullus' *Poem* 5, and certainly in *Patrick's Hymn*, W. Stokes and J. Strachan, *Thesaurus Palaeohibernicus*, vol. 2 (Cambridge 1903), p. 357.
44. Hesiod *Works and Days* 39, 221, 264.
45. As far as I know, Ben Jonson is the first modern to have made the comparison between Archilochus and the Irish poets in his *Poetaster*, 160-65.

46. W. Shakespeare, *As You Like It*, III, 2; it is also mentioned by Sir Philip Sidney, John Donne and others.

47. As recorded in the *Annals of the Four Masters:* D. Plunket Barton, *Links between Ireland and Shakespeare* (Dublin/London 1919), p. 64.

48. E.g., G. L. Kitteredge describes how in the sixteenth and seventeenth century educated men in England, including the most distinguished jurists, accepted easily the notion of witchcraft: 'English Witchcraft and James the First', in *Toy*, pp. 1-65.

49. *Dánta Aodhagain Ui Rathaille*, Irish Texts Soc. (1911) XXX: he is said to have killed a man by his satire, but it is clear that much of his poetry of attack left his enemies unmoved.

50. *Duanaire Dhaibhidh Ui Bhruadair*, edited by J. MacErlean, Irish Texts Soc. (1913), XXXI.

51. *Odyssey* 6, 184-85; 471-81.

52. Diodorus V, 31.2; Vendryes 95; Mercier, p. 109.

53. The spell-like character can clearly be seen:

cen colt for crib [cerníne]	without food quickly in a dish
cen gert ferrba fora n-assa athirni	without a cow's milk whereon a calf grows
cen adba fir fer druba diserche	without a man's abode under the gloom of night
cen dil dami resi rob sen Brisi	without paying a company of story tellers, let that be Bres' condition!

'and there was nothing but lassitude on that man from that time' from W. Stokes, *Revue Celtique* 12 (1891) 52-130; cf. Elliot, *Power*, p. 38; Hendrickson, pp. 124-25; J. Travis, *PMLA* 57 (1942) 909-915.

54. E. Ziebarth, *RE* s.v. 'Fluch'; J. H. Mozley, 'On Cursing in Ancient Times', appendix to Ovid, *The Art of Love and Other Poems* (Loeb Classical Library, London 1947).

55. Quoted by Mercier, pp. 148 f.

56. W. Stokes, 'The Wooing of Luaine and the Death of Athirne', *Revue Celtique* 24 (1903) 270-87; Elliott, *Power*, p. 27.

57. *Idyll* 2.

58. D. Hyde, *Abhráin atá leagtha ar an Reachtuíre* (Dublin 1903), p. 16.

59. F. N. Robinson, 'Satirists and Enchanters in Early Irish Literature' in *Toy*, p. 99.

60. M. L. West, *Hesiod, Theogony* (Oxford 1966), pp. 9-10; 14-15.

61. Julio Caro Baroja, 'Honour and Shame, A Historical Account of Several Conflicts', translated by R. Johnson, in *Honour and Shame*, pp. 79-137 (esp pp. 85 f.).

62. Sophocles shows Ajax (*Aias* 666-90) attempting to rationalize away his sense of dishonour by means of the characteristically Greek argument from the balance and rhythm of the natural world's changes. The argument fails to help him and his self-destructive desire prevails.

63. *Odyssey* 11, 271-80: she hanged herself for grief: Eustathius in *Od* 1684.

64. Sophocles, *Oedipus Tyrannus* 1060-61.

65. J. G. Frazer, *The Golden Bough*, Part IX, p. 19 referring to Euripides *El* 327.

66. Ibid., Part IV, pp. 44-49, 141, 220; Aeschines *In Ctesiphontem* 244.

67. B. Bohannan, *African Homicide and Suicide* (Princeton 1960), p. xxx mentions the custom of the injured person killing himself before the door of his offender. For suicide in the ancient world see Thalheim, *RE* s.v. Selbstmord; R. Hirzel, *Der Selbstmord* (Darmstadt 1968, reprint), who, significantly for our theme, quotes (p. 16 n. 2) a number of examples of Greek women who killed themselves on account of shame.

68. Chapter 2, the section on Neoboule.

CHAPTER 5

1. Love was a theme in Mimnermus' poetry: M was probably later than Archilochus, but his poems to his 'Nanno' hint that there was a developed tradition of expressing sexual love in poetry before his time.

2. Hauvette, pp. 194-95, 209.

3. Chapter 2 n. 74.

4. Chapter 2 n. 91.

5. *Ad Atticum* 2, 21, 4.

6. Marcuse, pp. 11 ff.

7. Mary C. Swabey, *Comic Laughter, A Philosophical Essay*, (Yale 1961) and D. H. Monro, *Argument of Laughter* (Melbourne) tend to emphasize the use of humour and its physical manifestation together as a regulator operating to effect the restoration of logic in an irrational context; Bergson's famous work *Le Rire* (Paris 1908) and Freud's *Jokes and Their Relation to the Unconscious* (Standard Edition, vol. 8) take a different view. Nobody has produced a viable definition of humour or wit.

8. Marcuse pp. 178-79.

9. 'Crazy Jane and the Bishop': W. B. Yeats, *Collected Poems* (London 1950) p. 290.

10. As is arguably the case in certain novels of D. H. Lawrence.

11. 199 T: φῦμα μηρῶν μεταξύ.

12. Horace *Epodes* 8, 5-6.

13. The word has both secular and religious connotations, see article βλασφημέω in Liddell-Scott-Jones.

14. Chapter 1 n. 40.

15. B. Snell, *The Discovery of Mind*, translated by Rosenmeyer (Oxford 1953), pp. 227 f.; R. S. Bluck, *Plato's Phaedo, a translation with introduction, notes and appendices* (London 1955), pp. 174 f.

16. See especially *Cratylus* 423 e-424b.

17. G. Steiner, *After Babel, Aspects of Language and Translation* (London 1975), pp. 36-39.

18. Marcuse, p. 15.

19. See the discussion of the newly discovered Cologne poem below.

20. F. Will, 'Archilochus and his senses', *CJ* (1961) 289-96 (esp p. 291).

21. This prompts his speech of *Iliad* I, 225-244, in which he protects his injured honour-image by swearing, with ritual accompaniment of an ἀδύνατον example (the possible sprouting into leaf of a bronze-bound staff) not to fight for the Greek army. Of course Agamemnon's main concern is that he should not be shamed as king by being left without a prize when Chryseis was returned to her father. The Trojan war, we must recall, was started to avenge the breach of Menelaus and his family's honour caused by the love of Helen and Paris.

22. Walcot, p. 74.

23. Julian Pitt-Rivers, 'Honour and Social Status' in *Honour and Shame*, pp. 68 ff.

24. *Iliad* 14, 190-221; 277-351.

25. *Od.* 8, 267-358.

26. Poseidon agrees to pay the adultery fine on Ares' behalf, an offer which Hephaistos cannot refuse: *Od.* 8, 347-358.

27. *Iliad* 24, 130-132.

28. *Theogonia* 603-7.

29. Hesiod *Works and Days* p. 374.

30. There is no certain interpretation of this interesting compound but most scholars agree that the πυγ-part of it represents the woman's hips. Probably some emphasis upon her hips either in her gait or the arrangement of her dress is indicated. A Κόρη found on the acropo-

lis, probably of about 525 B.C., and of island origin, shows how an archaic beauty, by delicate manipulation of her finely woven peplos, could make it accurately follow the contours of her hips and legs. This specimen, in G. M. A. Richter, *Korai, Archaic Greek Maidens*, (London 1968) illustrations nos. 561-7, probably represents the degree of flirtatious boldness A. has in mind. The skill of managing a peplos gracefully was the mark of a lady: Sappho fg. 70; quoted by Richter, p. 10.

31. Strepsiades' speech, *Nubes* 42-80.

32. There is no evidence about the type or identity of these statues; they do not represent goddesses or priestesses, nor do they represent the dedicator to the gods, for they were sometimes offered by men. Possibly they were offered as a symbolic female servant to the deity. (Richter, p. 3).

33. Cephisodorus, in his commentary on Aristotle: Athenaeus, 3, 94, 122b (cf. comm on 46 T).

34. Aristophanes *Lysistrate* 1119.

35. Diogenes Laertius 3, 35; F. Decleva-Caizzi, *Antisthenis Fragmenta* (Milan 1966), fg. 36.

36. Accepting Adrados' restoration of line 5 (quoted by Tarditi, in *Archilochus)*.

37. Lasserre's suggestion (cf. L/B 38).

38. Catullus 5; 8, 5.

39. Schol Aristophanes *Pax* 1148 (204 Dübner).

40. Plutarch *De Is. et Osir.* 365a; E. R. Dodds, Euripides' *Bacchae*, (Oxford 1944) pp. ix-x.

41. Ninck, pp. 28-29; F. M. Cornford, *Plato's Cosmology, The Timaeus of Plato* (London 1937), p. 259; R. B. Onians, *The Origins of European Thought* (Cambridge 1951), pp. 118 ff.

42. Heraclitus, Diels-Kranz 31; Clemens Alexandrinus *Strom.* v. 105; Ninck p. 29 n. 2.

43. These which can be related to the *Epodes* were more likely to be directed at the Lycambes family.

44. Cf. his rude expression for having sexual intercourse with a woman: [γυναῖ]κα βινέων 143 T.

45. Langerbeck; M. L. West, *Iambi et Elegi Graeci*, vol. 2 (Oxford 1972), pp. 74-75.

46. Livy I, 56.

47. O. Ribbeck, 'Über den Begriff des Eiron', *RhM* 31 (1876) 381-400.

48. Evidence that αὐλίσκος (diminutive of αὐλός, 'flute') could mean αἰδοῖον is found in Ptolemy Mathematicus (2nd century A.D.) but the equation probably antedates this period. The *Etymologicum Magnum* records that αὐλός was the name of a position of sexual intercourse.

49. Wilamowitz, 'Lesefrüchte', *Hermes* 33 (1898) 513-33 (p. 515) on the reading ἔμυζε for ἔβρυζε.

50. See Schol Aristophanes *Knights* 364-65 (on κύβδα); Liebel, p. 67; Wilamowitz, *Hermes* 59 (1924) 270-72 (p. 271); R. Lattimore, *AJP* (1944) 172-75 thinks that the allusion is not necessarily of this kind; so too F. Wolf, p. 132; Lasserre, p. 150; Grassman, p. 3 takes the view that there is a reference to fellatio (and in particular to Horace *Epode* 8, 20: *ore adlaborandum erit tibi*); cf. Rankin *GB*, p. 330.

51. Eusebius *Praep. Ev.* 5, 30—he lost his property through πολιτικὴ φλυαρία, his absurd political activities (literally 'political drivelling'): probably this does not refer simply to political or propagandist poetry (which might have caused his exile, possibly confiscation of property or a fine) but specifically to political activities of which his ψόγος was a part.

52. These words may be assembled into an iambic trimeter-catalectic: παχεῖα δῆμος ἐργάτις μυσάχνη: F. R. Adrados, 'Nouveaux Fragments et Interprétations d'Archiloque', *Revue de Philologie* 30 (1956) 28-36.

53. 42 L/B, line 6 (63 T).

54. Cf. 61 T.

55. *Col. Pap.* 18-24.

56. Chapter 6 of Lasserre is concerned with fragments to which much of Horace *Epode* 8 offers comparison; also F. Wolf's discussion, pp. 129-38.

57. 259 L/B; Rankin, *GB*, p. 330.

58. 236 T; 309 L/B; Rankin, op. cit.; Taillardat, p. 75, notes as well as plant metaphors for vagina, some animal names, χοῖρος, ὕσσαξ (fig), etc. and in particular a bird, χελιδών (swallow); also Diogenes Laertius 2, 116.

59. Cf. Taillardat, pp. 75-76.

60. V. Buchheit, 'Feigensymbolik im antiken Epigramm', *RhM* 103 (1960) 200-229.

61. 91 L/B; 118 T; v. 1 is a possible reconstruction by Lasserre deduced from introductory phrases in the prose of Nicetas and Aelian who quote the second line.

62. 71 D, 72 D; 71 B, 72 B; 89 L/B, 90 L/B; for discussion 71 B, 72 B; T. S. Duncan *WUS* (1920) 19-37; F. Will, *CJ* (1962) 289-96.

63. θιγεῖν with the accusative would be unusual, but Lasserre represents χεῖρα as the subject of θιγεῖν; in spite of this idea of tenderness rather than violence (a possible implication of θιγεῖν) seems reasonable; on this point, see H. Della Casa, 'Vindiciae Archilochiae, Lanx Satira Nicolao Terzaghi oblata', *Miscellanea Philologica, Pubblicazioni dell'Istituto di Filologia Classica e Medioevale* 16 (Genova 1963), 105-112 (p. 107).

64. Archilochus' version of a τόπος of erotic poetry: see the examples, Tarditi's commentary ad loc.

65. The juxtaposition of tenderness and violence, however objectionable it may seem to certain tastes (Duncan, op. cit. note 62, pp. 70-72), nevertheless seems quite in character for Archilochus, see the Cologne fragment below.

66. 25, 1-2; 25, 2-3D; 29, 1-2; 29, 2-3 B; 40, 1-2; 40, 2-3 L/B.

67. Synesius, *Phalakr. Enkom.* 75 b-c, says that the tress of hair 'is on the body of a whore'; Bergk was probably the first to regard it as a description of Neoboule; for discussion, see Marzullo and Costanza. L/B commentary on fg. 40 L/B suggest that Synesius may have misinterpreted the poet's words.

68. Costanza, p. 156.

69. In spite of the explicitness of Synesius, it remains possible that he had only a portion of the poet's work before him; there is much therefore in favour of L/B's support of the hypothesis that Neoboule is involved in this fragment. However, his comment is sufficiently clear for the present discussion. Perhaps Archilochus was describing a κόρη statue? See Costanza, pp. 160 ff. and note 28 above.

70. Costanza, p. 161.

71. For the erotic significance of long hair in Greece: Marzullo, pp. 73 ff.

72. 27 T (38 L/B). See L/B notes on 38 (p. 14) combining *Pap. Ox.* 2311 fr 1 with these two verses quoted by Athenaeus 688c.

73. Cf. ὕσσαξ, χοῖρος, etc. for vagina in Aristophanes; see note 59 above.

74. Rankin *Eranos* (1974); see the discussion of this poem in chapter 6 below.

75. Three commentaries on this poem are available at the time of this writing: Merkelbach and West, Marcovich, and Marzullo, *Museum Criticum* 8/9 (1973–74) 32-92. The issue of *Museum Criticum* (hereafter *Mus. Cr.*) also contains a number of valuable contributions by other scholars to the discussion of the poem. For brief notes on the question of the poem's authenticity, see the Appendix to this work. Note that I agree with Merkelbach and West and others in regarding the girl in this poem to be the younger sister of Neoboule; J. Ebert and W. Luppe argue (*ZPE* 16 [1975] 23-33) that some other girl is meant.

76. Merkelbach and West, *ZPE* 14 (1974) 97-113.

77. In this 'translation' rounded brackets ( ) indicate supplementary suggestions, explanations and interpretations of the text; squared brackets [ ] indicate suggestions for missing text.

78. 'Dare to desire an equal (requited ?) love': so Merkelbach and West, Marcovich, and Marzullo interpret this text with minor variations. Gallavotti (*Mus. Cr.* p. 29) reads Ἴσον δὲ τολμηρῷ δοκέω': 'I think this is equal to something (over) daring'—presumably some kind of expression of shock or outrage (genuine or otherwise) on the part of the girl.

79. θυμός: 'spirit', 'will': Merkelbach and West suggest a possible *sensus obscaenus* of this word whereby it means 'penis'; cf. Hipponax fg. 10. Marzullo (*Mus. Cr.* p. 34) rejects this idea, as does Marcovich, who says such a pun would be out of character for a pure young girl who is directly contrasted with the aging, lascivious Neoboule.

80. Merkelbach and West interpretation: *alii alia*.

81. The poet need not be regarded as necessarily being very young on account of this phrase. He may well be recalling an incident of previous years, or making a general remark about 'young men' for ironical purposes. But as far as we know his life-span (chapter 2 above) he did not reach advanced middle age, let alone old age, and much of his work may be presumed to have been done when he was in the 'young man' age group. This incident is certainly in the past, or imagined so to be, see Barigazzi, *Mus. Cr.*, p. 9.

82. R. Kannicht's suggestion, reported by Merkelbach and West.

83. This is not tantamount to a proposal of marriage; it is more like a 'proposition', but cf. Merkelbach and West, and Marzullo's comments (*Mus. Cr.*, p. 46).

84. This seems to mean (reading πείσομαι or φείσομαι) that she has persuaded him to be content with less than complete sexual intercourse. E. Degani (*QUCC* 20 [1975] 229) has shown conclusively from a reference in a gloss of Hesychius that the phrase θεῖον χρῆμα (line 10) meant complete sexual union.

85. Merkelbach and West, Marcovich, and Marzullo (*Mus. Cr.* p. 50-51) mention various examples of the 'garden' metaphor for female pudenda, e.g. *Anth. Lat.* 885; Diogenes Laertius 2, 116; Aristophanes *Lysistrate* 88, *Aves* 507; cf. Taillardat, p. 75-76.

86. Or 'let not even the king of gods'—D. L. Page's suggestion reported in Merkelbach and West.

87. The respectable Greek female had a limited circle of acquaintances.

88. See Marzullo's comments (*Mus. Cr.*, p. 67) on this proverb.

89. An expression which reminds us of Neoboule, whose 'flower' has withered (line 18).

90. See the parallels and examples in Marzullo (*Mus. Cr.*, p. 76) which suggest that μαζῶν, breasts, should be read at the beginning of the line.

91. See Marzullo, *Mus. Cr.*, p. 77.

92. Barigazzi, *Mus. Cr.*, p. 5.

93. See Merkelbach and West; Marcovich, p. 14, suggests that *coitus interruptus* is meant; but possibly the poet is speaking of some kind of intercrural intercourse.

94. Cf. Catullus who protests about his virility in poem 16, and his account of his male prowess in his poem 32 about Ipsitilla—extreme examples amongst many in his work of a masculine assertiveness that presupposes a comprehending male audience.

95. Using Margaret Murray's phrase for her hypothesis of a submerged fertility religion of Europe, *The Witch Cult in Western Europe* (Oxford 1921), etc.

CHAPTER 6

1. Bearing in mind the tentative nature of our inferences concerning these.

2. 54 T: *Pap. Ox.* 2310 14-16; cf. 104 T; Rankin, *Eranos*, p. 6 n. 12.

3. 10 T; 12 T.

4. See Wolf; *Col. Pap.*, see discussion in chapter 5 above.

5. Eusebius *Praep. Ev.* 5 30.

6. Rankin, in *GB* and *Emerita* (1975).

7. Athenaeus 627 c.
8. Plato *Republic* 412 b ff; Guthrie, vol. 4, pp. 461 ff.
9. See W. G. Forrest's discussion, *The Emergence of Greek Democracy*, pp. 46 ff; W. Donlan, *Historia* 22 (1973) 145-54.
10. *Iliad* 2, 212-52.
11. Rankin, *Symbolae Osloenses*, pp. 36-60.
12. *Odyssey* 5, 184-5.
13. Chapter 3, notes 60, 61; chapter 4 n. 42 and especially A. Parry, *TAPA* 87 (1956) 1-7 and Hauvette, pp. 206, 209.
14. 193 T (79 D): *P. Argent* 3: The poet wishes some foe to be carried off by the waves and eventually seized by fierce Thracian tribesmen, then to have many woes 'eating the bread of slavery'; he wants to see him shivering, with sea-weed hanging from his body, gnashing his teeth like a dog lying in extremities at the edge of the sea—that is what he wishes for the man who betrayed him, and who previously was his friend.
15. N. Kontoleon, *Entretiens*, pp. 37-86 (esp p. 39).
16. Fränkel, *Dichtung*, p. 186.
17. τοῖος ἀνθρώποισι θυμός, Γλαῦκε,
    Λεπτινέω παῖ
    γίνεται θνητοῖσ', ὁκοίην Ζεὺς ἐφ' ἡμέρην ἄγῃ
    'Mortal men's mind, Glaukos son of Leptines, is
    like whatever day Zeus brings.' Cf. *Od* 18, 136-7.
18. 102T: οὐ τις αἰδοῖος μετ' ἀστῶν ⟨οὐδὲ⟩ περίφημος θάνων
    γίνεται· χάριν δὲ μᾶλλον τοῦ ζοοῦ διώκομεν
    –ζοοί· κάκιστα δ'αἰει τῷ θανόντι γίνεται
    'nobody becomes respected amongst his fellow citizens nor
    distinguished by dying; we seek the favour of the living man,
    for we are alive. The worst abuse is always for the man who is dead.'
19. *Iliad* 18, 458 ff., e.g. Achilles' destiny to be short-lived but of glorious memory.
20. Chapter 2 notes 101, 102.
21. Cf. Rankin, *Eranos*, pp. 1-15.
22. Chapter 2 n. 164.
23. Perhaps κακοστομέειν, 'abuse', should complete this line: E. Lobel, and C. H. Roberts, *Oxyrhynchus Papyri* (London 1954); F. Adrados, *PP* (1955–56) 38-48; W. Peek, *Philologus* 99 (1955) 193-219; other suggestions by other scholars, all along these lines, are noted by Rankin, in *Eranos*, p. 5, n. 9.
24. Following here, as in most of this text, the text of the poem put forward by M. L. West, *Iambi et Elegi Graeci Ante Alexandrum Cantati* (Oxford 1971), fgs 23, 24. The words within square [ ] brackets are restorations. In the English rendering which follows, the words within rounded brackets ( ) are supplements or interpretations.
25. For an account of arguments for and against, see Rankin in *Eranos*, op. cit. who takes the view that one poem with different phrases or movements is represented by the surviving verses.
26. Omitting material too fragmentary to make sense.
27. The addressee is probably Neoboule, see 35 L/B, Treu, pp. 182-84; A. Giannini, *Acme* 11 (1958) 91-6 (esp p. 45). Adrados, *PP* 41 (1955–56) 38-48 (esp p. 40) rejects the idea that Neoboule is involved here, but thinks it is some other woman.
28. μύρμηξ is probably the proverbial ant who, though weak and feeble, eventually turned to resist. So Lobel, who convincingly restored this word in the papyrus text. For discussion, see Rankin *Eranos*, p. 4 n. 6. Also, O. Lendle 'Archilochos Politischer Ratgeber seiner Mitbürger' in *Politeia und Respublica Palingenesia IV Beiträge zum Verständnis von Politik, Recht und Staat in der Antike* (Wiesbaden 1969) *dem Andenken Rudolf Starks gewidmet*, pp. 39-51 for the view that Myrmex is the name of a general.

29. A new phase begins here, possibly involving the representation by the poet of an oracle which has actually or in his fantasy addressed him about his future.

30. Archilochus seems to have been the first in our surviving literature to use the foreign word τυραννίς (22 T) or its variant τυραννίη which we find here. It may be noted that the concept is well established in A's time; see further Gallavotti, *PP* 10 (1949) 69-71: H. Berve, *Die Tyrannis bei den Griechen*, vol. 1 (Munich 1967), pp. 9 f; Busolt, *Griechische Staatskunde* 1, pp. 381 ff; D. Hegyi, 'Notes on the Origin of Greek Tyrannis', *A Ant Hung* 11 (1965) 303-318.

31. On the question of whether this line represents a transition within the poem or the beginning of a new one: Peek, *Philologus* 99 (1955) 193-219 (esp p. 197) for the 'separatist' view: Rankin *Eranos*, p. 10, *contra*.

32. It is barely possible that we should read here [γά]μοισιν ἐξ[η ρτυμένοι]ς 'for the marriage having been arranged?' As L/B suggest, 'pour les noces déjà preparées'. Other suggestions include ὀφθαλμοῖσιν 'for the eyes', στολμοῖσιν 'expeditions', etc., etc.; see Rankin, *Eranos*, p. 11 n. 29.

33. Rankin *Eranos*, pp. 12-13.

34. A. J. Graham, *Colony and Mother City in Ancient Greece* (Manchester 1964), pp. 72 ff.

35. E.g. 6 T: ξείνια δυσμενέεσσι λυγρὰ χαριζόμενοι: 'doing our enemies the favour of bitter gifts'; 14 T κρύπτωμεν <δ'> ἀνιηρὰ Ποσειδάωνος ἄνακτος / δῶρα 'let us conceal the terrible gifts of the lord Poseidon'.

36. Most of these phenomena appear to be indicated in the (itself mutilated) tetrameter fragment 99 T.

37. R. Pfeiffer, 'Gottheit und Individuum in der frühgriechischen Lyrik', *Philologus* (84) 137-52 (esp. p. 140).

38. 100 T and (perhaps) 149 T.

39. See the discussion in chapter 2 above in the section, *The Eclipse*.

40. G. Lanata, *QUCC* 6 (1968) 33-35.

41. Thucydides 8: 53, 63, 75 ff.

42. 22 T 4.

43. Aristotle *Rhet.* 1418 b 28.

44. As in fg 96 T where the ugly but effective στρατηγός is preferred. Cf. fg 95 T's uncomplimentary reference to Glaucos; and chapter 3 notes 39 and 40 above.

45. Cf. F. Will's discussion, *Archilochus* TWAS series, (New York 1960) chapter 4.

CHAPTER 7

1. See Maas, *Greek Metre*.

2. Maas, p. 21; Watkins, pp. 194-249; West, *Glotta*, pp. 161-87, West, *CQ*, pp. 179-92.

3. Maas, pp. 8, 41; Watkins, pp. 197-98; West, *CQ*, p. 181.

4. Maas, p. 93; A. D. Knox, *Philologus* 87 (1932) 19-39.

5. It seems reasonable to regard Callinus as somewhat earlier than Archilochus: so Schmid-Stählin, I i, p. 357; Lesky, p. 108; the most significant ancient evidence being Strabo 647 and Didymus, περὶ ποιητῶν, Schmid p. 387 (L/B p. civ). I think it important that, as Strabo points out, Callinus speaks of the Magnesians as a still flourishing state, whereas Archilochus speaks of their destruction. This is not entirely conclusive, but I think Dover underestimates this Strabo passage somewhat where he argues (*Entretiens*, p. 193) that they were contemporary. G. Geiger, *De Callini Elegiarum Scriptoris Aetate* (Erlangen 1877) also thinks them contemporary.

6. Maas, p. 52; Dover, *Entretiens*, p. 189.

7. Chapter 2 notes 37 and 74.

8. Watkins, pp. 209-10.

9. Chapter 3 note 5.

10. Watkins, and West, op. cit. note 2 above.
11. Watkins, pp. 196-98.
12. Watkins, p. 195.
13. Cf. chapter 2 note 74; Clemens Alexandrinus *Strom.* 1. 16. 79; possibly—depending on whether *repertor* is 'inventor' or 'deviser'—Ovid *Ibis* 519-20; *utque repertori nocuit pugnacis iambi/sic sit in exitium lingua proterva tuum.*
14. A. E. Harvey, 'The Classification of Greek Lyric Poetry', *CQ* 5 (1955) 157-75.
15. But see Dover's discussion, *Entretiens*, pp. 188 ff.
16. C. M. Bowra, *Early Greek Elegists* (Cambridge reprint 1960), pp. 12-16.
17. Fg 3 D: νῦν δ'ἐπὶ Κιμμερίων στρατὸς ἔρχεται ὀβριμοεργῶν 'but now there approaches the army of the K. who do dread deeds' (Strabo 647).
18. Chapter 3 note 46.
19. Stobaeus 4, 56 classifies the *consolatio* to Pericles (10 T, 1 L/B) amongst the παρηγορικά.
20. See chapter 3 above.
21. Fg 6 T.
22. 12 T (3 L/B), 14 T (4 L/B): Philostratus *De Poet. Aud.* 23 ab.
23. The writer on 'The Sublime' 10, 7 on the poem to Pericles.
24. 11 T: πολλὰ δ'εὐπλοκάμου πολιῆς ἁλὸς ἐν πελάγεσσι/θεσσάμενοι γλυκερὸν νόστον: 'in the seas of long tressed grey salt water praying for a happy homecoming'.
25. 7 T, 87 T, possibly 63 T: F. J. Cuartero, 'La metáfora de la nave de Arquiloco a Esquilo', *BIEH* 11. 2 (1968) 41-45.
26. V. Ehrenberg, *CP* 57 (1962) 239-40; Gentili, pp. 129-34; Rankin *Emerita* (1972), pp. 469-74.
27. Gentili, pp. 129-34.
28. Chapter 3 note 41 above.
29. Cf. R. Lattimore, *Themes in Greek and Latin Epitaphs* (Urbana 1962), chapter 8: 'Biographical Themes'.
30. *Odyssey* 5 196: chapter 3 note 4 above.
31. See the discussion in chapter 6 above.
32. 15 T (attributed to Archilochus by Bergk); 38 T.
33. Cf. 280 T, see also L/B 266-70; Dio Chrysostomus *Orat* 60; schol Apollonius Rhodius 1, 1212; schol Ven B Homer *Iliad* 22, 237: there may be a hint of a kind of proto-dramatic dialogue in his *Epodes*; cf. *Col. Pap.* discussed in chapter 5 above.
34. *RE* s.v. Archilochus (Crusius) for various figures of speech and stylistic devices. We may note as examples: Archilochus has 'etymological' figures: 30 T, 115 T (repetition in prayer formula), and in 55 T a remarkable polyptoton. He is fond of onomatopoeic expressions: 29 T ἐμυζε(ἐβρυζε); 32 T βάβαξ; 36 T ἀπέφλυσαν; possibly in 2 T the repetition of the phrase ἐν δορί may involve a kind of syntactical pun.
35. 88 T: Πανελλήνων ὀϊζὺς ἐς Θάσον συνέδραμεν: 'the wretchedness of all Greece ran together (to meet) in Thasos'.
36. Cuartero, op. cit. note 25; Gerlach, pp. 128 ff.
37. 109 T; 111 T; 112 T; 139 T (?).
38. 111 T; 112 T.
39. Wolf, p. 2
40. 168 T, 169 T, 171 T, etc.; for a suggested reconstruction: L/B 159-176 (pp. 49 ff.) and Lasserre, *Les Epodes.*
41. *RE* s.v. Archilochus (Crusius) I 1029: *RE* s.v. 'Fabel' (Hausrath); B. E. Perry, *Aesopica* (Illinois 1952), pp. 52, 65, 71-72, 101.
42. Hesiod *Works and Days* 201 ff.
43. E.g. 43 T, the βοῦς ἐργάτης, and the μύρμηξ, 54 T, possibly refer to fables rather than proverbs. On the significance of animals as examples in Greek cultural tradition, see Grant, *Folk-Tale* etc.; G. M. Sifakis, *Parabasis and Animal Choruses, A Contribution to the History of Attic Comedy* (London 1971), pp. 65, 79.

44. See the notes in Tarditi, *Archilochus*.

45. See Thompson; E. Kallos 'Gloses pour Archiloque', *A Ant Hung* 1 (1951) 67-74.

46. Thompson, p. 19.

47. F. W. Lenz, 'The Monkeys of Archilochus', *AJP* 66 261 (1945) 34-49.

48. Rankin *Emerita*, pp. 249-55.

49. Grant, p. 18.

50. See Appendix, note 1 below.

51. See Appendix below.

52. See the discussion in chapter 5 above.

53. Stanza: Iambic trimeter + Hemiepes + Iambic Dimeter: an epodic verse form; Merkelbach and West, p. 102.

54. M. S. Silk, *Interaction in Poetic Imagery* (Cambridge 1974), p. 185.

55. But we would do well always to bear in mind that our impressions are inevitably focused and restricted in the case of an individual fragment of papyrus by the 'selectivity of historical chance' which has allowed one phrase, word, or group to survive and others to be lost; just as we are influenced by the 'selectivity of quotation' in literary sources, whereby authors in a given period were attracted by and so quoted certain types of material. This is quite apart from the relative popularity of authors at different periods, which affects the availability of texts to be quoted or to be candidates for survival either in manuscript or papyrus; e.g., H. Kenner in his introduction to Davenport's *Archilochus*, p. viii: 'By a kind of inspired syncopation, the rip in the ms does not conveniently excise the bawdy word, but instead, the words just after it. . . .'

56. Words of Sappho, possibly intended by Pound in his version to constitute a satire upon the 'imagist' poets. This fragment of Sappho is now regarded as part of a longer fragmentary poem from Sappho Bk E: Edgar Lobel and D. L. Page, *Poetarum Lesbiorum Fragmenta* (Oxford 1955) fg. 95. Gongyla was evidently a friend of Sappho: she may be mentioned at fg 22 (L and P) and certainly appears in fg 213, 6. Pound evidently derived his inspiration from the first few lines which appeared in J. M. Edmonds' *New Fragments of Alcaeus, Sappho and Corinna* (London 1909); see Collinge, *Notes and Queries* (June 1956), p. 265. also K. K. Ruthwen, *A Guide to Ezra Pound's Personae* (California 1969), pp. 190-91.

57. Davenport, op. cit.

58. Davenport, p. vii.

59. Will, op. cit. (chapter 6 note 45).

THE NEW POEM AND CURRENT ARCHILOCHEAN CRITICISM

The Cologne papyrus is the subject of lively discussion in a continuous stream of publi-
cations, and it does not need oracular insight to predict that this flow will not dry up for
some time. Not only is the poem's authenticity debated, with a current majority (for what
that in itself is worth) in favour of its genuineness, but this discussion has led to the airing of
related Archilochean themes, indeed to the whole problem of how we should read and in-
terpret his poetry. I do not propose to give a comprehensive list of articles which have come
out since I finished the preceding chapters, nor of material which I did not know of or could
not obtain during their composition. I shall address myself instead to a few points made in
some of these publications, with emphasis upon those points that disagree with the view of
Archilochus which I have put forward.

Let me recommend as a source the number of *Arethusa* (vol. 9, No. 2, 1976) which has
been devoted to the new poem. It is full of vital and witty argument, and one of its most rep-
resentatively interesting items is Mary R. Lefkowitz's article 'Fiction in Literary Biography:
The New Poem and the Archilochus Legend' (pp. 181-89). I shall mention briefly what seem
to me to be main relevant points of this article which combines brevity with acuteness. I
hope to discuss the questions which it raises at greater length at some other time. I agree
entirely with her that the poem is genuinely Archilochean. In the following remarks the
whole numbers refer to Dr. Lefkowitz's views and those with decimals my comments upon
them.

1. She regards Critias' account of the poet as derived mostly from his poetry and
having no independent biographical value: Critias' critical premise is that the man and his
poetry are synonymous (p. 183).

1.1. On the whole, I agree, but it is, I think, a reasonable view that from a poet who
expresses himself in the first person (whatever roles or masks he may put over it from time to
time) you can expect to learn something of his own point of view, and not infrequently, of
his actual life and experience. So unless the ceremonial, ritual origin of iambic, the 'struc-
ture' if you wish, is predominant in moulding the contents, and there is no hard evidence for
this, then A. can be supposed sometimes to tell us something about himself. This is different
from regarding the man and his poetry as synonymous.

1.2. Critias knew the body of Greek poetry, and the nuances and semantic sinuosi-
ties of the Greek language in a way that none of us can. Like others of his class and time he
was deeply learned in poetry of various genres. Learning large quantities of poetry by heart
was a staple of the education of such men as Critias (Plato *Protagoras* 325e-326a).

1.3. The surviving passage of Critias on Archilochus tells us of an aspect of the poet
that especially impressed the author, namely the unashamed exposure of all the disgraceful
or discreditable aspects of his own life. We have no grounds for considering Critias' reading
of the poet as so naive that he could not discern the personal note and the strange perverse
piece of factual information in a matrix of poetic utterance formed and blended (but hardly
rigidified) by an artistic convention. Critias made many wrong decisions during his life and
some of them were disastrous. He was also a skilled rhetorician and publicist. He was not in-
variably scrupulous. But he was no fool.

2. According to Dr. Lefkowitz (p. 183), Pindar, considerably earlier in the fifth century B.C., also identified poet and poetry in his references to Archilochus (Pindar *Pythian* 2. 54-5). This identification is as Dover suggests, 'a post-archaic development, a consequence of the new literary and international communication that was expedited after the Persian Wars, when the old lyric mimesis had become obsolete and its technique had been forgotten'. (Dover, *Entretiens*,p. 211).

2.1. Pindar was born around 518 B.C. He was undoubtedly an adult by the time of the Persian Wars, (490–479 B.C. approx.) and is a product of late 'Archaic' rather than 'Classical' Greece. Apart from Heraclitus, he is the oldest of those who refer to Archilochus. If there is a significant difference between 'pre Wars' Greek culture and that which followed, there can hardly be any doubt that of all people this man, with his great feeling for tradition in many aspects of life, would retain his awareness of the older ways of looking at poetry.

2.2. But there is no evidence for a cultural cleavage of the kind mentioned, dividing poetry into two phases. Nor does Dover say so in the way that Dr. L. does, for he expresses himself rather more cautiously on this matter (see *Entretiens*, especially pp. 211-13). There is no sign of a communications revolution. Even the spread of written literature was not so significant as all that.

2.3. By profession, and because he belonged to a family which had contacts all over the Greek world, Pindar was likely to know about a wide variety of poetic conventions and types. He is not likely to have been misled by his misunderstanding of what Archilochus was saying or how he was saying it.

3. Dr. Lefkowitz discounts the inscriptions of Mnesiepes and Sosthenes as derived from the poet's works, associating them with the 'often incredible fiction of Hellenistic biography' (p. 183).

3.1. The story of the meeting with the Muses to which Dr. Lefkowitz refers in connection with her view of the inscriptions, is certainly paralleled by other stories of the original inspiration of poets and holy men (e.g. Hesiod, Isyllus or later, incidents on the road to Damascus and the road to Emmaus). In the ancient world people tended to visualize decisive points in their lives in this kind of way, whether waking or in dream (see E. R. Dodds, *The Greeks and the Irrational* [Calif. 1951] passim). The story was known quite early in the fifth century B.C., to judge from its apparent occurrence on a piece of pottery (Kontoleon, *Arkh Eph*; Parke *CQ* 1958). The story is irrelevant to the question of the extent to which the inscriptions are fictional or the extent to which they may have been derived from Archilochus' poetry—which is a separate question.

3.2. On the first of these questions, it is at least as likely that local tradition preserved factual information about the poet's life independently of the poet's own utterances in the poems themselves as that the inscriptions were entirely derived from his poems. We have here inscriptions associated with a local hero in his own island, a hero whose memory is elaborately revered. There is a difference between this situation and the obviously concocted lives of Homer and others which Dr. L. adduces in this connection (pp. 184-85).

3.3. We should need to be possessed of much more of Archilochus' poetry in order to be quite sure about the second of these questions.

3.4. Mythopoeia, which certainly characterizes the incriptional account of the poet's life, is inclusive of fact rather than exclusive. It is a modality of expression and not simply the expression of non-facts. Irish mythopoeia has made Jonathan Swift into a mythic hero and stories such as Diarmuid MacCoiter's 'An Déin Swift agus Sean Bocht' place him in strange fictional circumstances which nevertheless reflect historically well known facts about him: his efforts to benefit his fellow countrymen, his fondness for walking about the country and conversing with people, and his sympathy for women (see J. K. Walton, 'The Unity of the Travels', *Hermathena* 104 [1967] 5-50).

4. Dr. Lefkowitz asks why we should think that the girl in the poem is Neoboule's sister.

4.1. It seems reasonable that she should be some close connection on the same social level, and certainly not a slave. The fragment mentioning a sister, 24 T, may be the clue that others have thought it to be. Also references in the testimonia to sisters need not be completely irrelevant.

5. With T. Gelzer (*Poetica* 6 [1974] 490) Dr. Lefkowitz asks why the name Amphimedo does not occur in the testimonia about Archilochean life.

5.1. If these testimonia are as derivative from the poems as Dr. Lefkowitz argues, then it does not matter much whether or not the name occurs.

5.2. We would only expect the name to occur if the testimonia were comprehensive, and they are not.

6. Parallels between the story of Lycambes and that of Bupalus, the supposed victim of Hipponax's satire, and that of Telestagoras of Naxos who was destroyed with his daughters by the insults of a *komos* of young men against them (Aristotle fg 558), are held by Dr. Lefkowitz not to 'prove that the Lycambes story is unauthentic, just that it is unhistorical' (p. 188).

6.1. It can never be decided with scientific rigour whether Lycambes was historical or not. All that these parallels ultimately prove is the fear in Archaic Greece of satire's ability to destroy 'honour', and (possibly) life as a consequence.

6.2. All this is ultimately a matter of literary judgement. The nature of the evidence does not admit conclusive demonstration. I happen to disagree with some viewpoints in this article, but I respect them none the less. My reading of Archilochus suggests to me most strongly that the power and the vitality of this poet, which were recognised as quite extraordinary in antiquity and which stare at one with such acerbity and uncompromising force from his fragmentary works, were not deployed against stock figures (whatever their names). I think that his description of human suffering in love and war tells us very clearly of his own, and that he, like Hesiod, reveals a considerable amount of his own life. He is not giving us an *emphemeris* like Ausonius. He gives us that essentially poetic benefit, an emotionally distilled and intensified vision of his experience of some of his life's incidents.

Scepticism about the identity and historicity of the Lycambids is noticeable in critical works which have followed the publication of the new poem. This note was first struck by Piccolomini in 1883, and it occurs in Gallavotti's article in 1949. The idea has been given its recent access of energy by a reaction to R. Merkelbach's opinion in 'Epilog eines der Herausgeber', *ZPE* 14 (1974) 173 that Archilochus was 'a vicious psychopath' in attacking the Lycambids in the way he did. It was not so much the notion that Archilochus was not a perfect gentleman that provoked scholarly opinion. It was Merkelbach's apparent literal acceptance of the tradition, especially in regard to the new poem. The historicity of the Lycambid story is criticised by M. L. West in 'Archilochus Ludens', *ZPE* 16 (1975) 217 ff. He criticised it also in *Studies in Greek Elegy and Iambus* (Berlin 1974) 25-27. So also E. Degani 'Il Nuovo Archiloco', *Atene e Roma* 19, 3-4 (1974) 113-128 (p. 123) and J. Van Sickle 'The New Erotic Fragment of Archilochus', *Quaderni Urbinati* 20 (1975) 123-156 (p. 151); also G. Nagy, *Arethusa* vol. 9, 191-206 (pp. 193-94) and Dr. Lefkowitz in her *Arethusa* article, pp. 184-85.

The main contention is that Iambic, taken in its broad sense and including metres other than pure iambs, is part of a ritual or ceremonial, and has origins in ritual worship. Part of the function of the verse in ritual is the castigation of vices and shortcomings, addressing stock figures and not real people.

This may be true, or it may not, of the early origins of the iambic mode. We have little evidence either way. It is hard to accept, however, that iambic should be so confined in some such an antique corset of 'structural' formality that it never developed beyond its supposed original function of being a medium of personally felt, personally directed feeling and opinion. Other genres of Greek poetry certainly did grow up to participate in the social and political life of the *polis*. Why should iambic remain as an example of arrested development?

I do not believe that Archilochus' fragments should be read in this way. I think he had real targets. Suppose that false names were used in his poetry, would it not be easy enough to do damage to individuals by using false names that they and others recognized as applying to them, as Catullus did with the unfortunate 'Mentula'?

However, the etymologies of names like Lycambes (involving 'wolf', etc.) or Neoboule ('girl who changes her mind') which have been adduced by Dr. West and others in support of the idea that there were no actual Lycambids, can hardly be very weighty evidence. What about Archilochus' own name, which means 'captain of a company'? Is he too the stock figure of the 'miles gloriosus' rejected in love? Wilamowitz in his *Platon* (Berlin 1920), vol. I, p. 93, recalls Boeckh's student who was excited by his discovery that Socrates' mother Phaenarete, has a name which means 'she who brings virtue into the light of day'. What could be more appropriate? And what less significant?

I have no doubt that debate on all these topics will proceed in coming years with such ferocity and vigour as will rejoice the shade of the poet himself.

English Index

Abantes, 22
Achilles, 45, 51, 52, 59, 76, 82
Adrados, F., 122
Aelian, 4, 11
Aeschines, 50
Agamemnon, 52, 56, 59
Aias (Ajax), 110
Aigisthus, 56
Alcaeus, 97
Alcidamas, 2, 5, 12, 50, 107
Alcman, 119
Amphidamas of Chalkis, 22
Amphimedo, 20
Anacreon, 4, 11, 44
Antidosis of Isocrates, 27
Antiphon, 12
Antisthenes, 61
Apelles, 58
Aphrodite, 60, 67
Apollo, 30, 48, 54
Apollodorus, the chronographer, 23, 25, 36
Apollonius of Rhodes, 6
Aratus, 96
Archilocheion, 2, 5, 16, 17, 50
Archilochoi of Cratinus, 3
Archilochus
    as poet and teacher, 8, 39
    attitude to society, 7, 38, 39
    attitude to war, 4, 10, 11, 21-22
    connection with Delphi and patronage of Apollo, 7, 16, 17
    Critias' opinion of him, 11
    elegies, 84, 85, 86, 87, 88, 89
    his biography by Demeas, 2
    his engagement to Neoboule, 19-20
    his social status, 8, 10, 12, 15
    metres, 85, 86, 87
    possible priestly associations of, 18
    possible service as mercenary soldier, 15, 16, 43, 76, 77
    significance of his name, 15
    techniques of composition, 38, 39
    traditional dates of his life, 22, 23, 25

Greek Index